LIVING *by the* BOOK

LIVING *by the* BOOK

Margaret Cundiff

Text of this edition copyright © Margaret Cundiff 1999

The author asserts the moral right
to be identified as the author of this work

Published by
The Bible Reading Fellowship
Peter's Way, Sandy Lane West
Oxford OX4 5HG
ISBN 1 84101 074 X

First published 1986 by Triangle/SPCK
This edition published 1999
10 9 8 7 6 5 4 3 2 1 0

Acknowledgments
Scriptures quoted from the Good News Bible published by The Bible Societies/
HarperCollins Publishers Ltd, UK © American Bible Society 1966, 1971, 1976, 1992,
used with permission.
Extracts from *The Alternative Service Book 1980* are copyright © The Archbishops'
Council of the Church of England 1980; The Archbishops' Council 1999
and are reproduced by permission.

A catalogue record for this book is available
from the British Library

Printed and bound in Great Britain
by Caledonian Book Manufacturing International, Glasgow

Contents

Preface

The train from Doncaster to Kings Cross sped swiftly through the uninteresting, flat countryside. Mile after mile of fields; just here and there were houses dotted about, and occasionally we went through stations, but were unable to read the names on the platforms, for this was the 'age of the train'—and high speed at that!

The train was full, mainly of business people, with briefcases open before them, some going through papers for meetings, others earnestly discussing an agenda, making plans of action, travelling as members of committees, groups, delegates. Some people had less serious plans: the shoppers, those going to meet up with friends, others with children having a day out to 'see London'.

With not much to interest us looking out of the window, and having fortified ourselves with cups of British Rail coffee, the people in my section of the carriage began to exchange pleasantries: about the weather, what was in the papers, the quality of the coffee. Then a sharing of confidences: where we were going, why, what time we would be coming back. After a while, seeing people were happy to talk, came the questions: 'How often do you come on this train?' 'Where do you stay in London?' and 'What's your job?'

The man opposite me asked, 'And what line of business are you in?' I'd noticed he had been trying to read my agenda papers upside-down and obviously wasn't making much headway!

I thought about the question. 'I suppose I'm in the risk business,' I said, tongue in cheek.

He looked puzzled, so I gave him a clue. 'I'm a deaconess in the

Church of England—a very risky business, a woman in the Church.'

He still looked puzzled. 'But who do you work for?'

'God,' I replied, and then went on to explain just what I did. It seemed to relax the people around me, anyway, and soon I was hearing about their families, their lives, and what they thought about religion.

The man in the corner hadn't said much, but had been obviously following everything with interest. 'I'm all for religion,' he said. 'It's a very good thing, a faith. If everybody lived by the Sermon on the Mount, the world would be a better place.'

'Yes,' I agreed. 'But the trouble is, how many people know where to find the Sermon on the Mount in the Bible? How many people even know what it says, or what the implications are for us today?'

That proved to be a 'lead balloon'—a real conversation stopper. I noticed one or two flushed faces, and an uneasy smile from my companion across the table, rather like children in class knowing that the teacher is going to ask someone a question, and hoping it won't be them.

I didn't pursue it; we were nearly at Kings Cross. We all gathered our belongings, and were soon going our separate ways, streaming out of the station.

Coming back that night, I refreshed my own memory of the Sermon on the Mount—after all, my friend of the morning might be getting on the train, although I didn't see him! As the train thundered back up to Doncaster I began to ponder. Although the words are so familiar, what do most people make of them today? People like my friends of the morning; the folk I meet every day who are full of good will, yet with only vague ideas of what Christianity is about; or even unquestioning church members. How can they live by those standards if they don't even know what they mean?

Then I suppose I pushed such thoughts to the back of my mind, but over the next few months they kept recurring. I found I was looking at the Sermon on the Mount with greater interest, asking myself questions, finding out what commentaries said, and what the people around me thought. Out of all that came the thought, 'Yes, if we all lived by The Book, we would indeed be different. I'd be different...' A serious and frightening thought! I remembered, too, my rather flippant reply to the question, 'And what line of business are you in?'—'The risk business.' All right, I said to myself, take the plunge. Stick your neck out, state what 'living by the Book' says to you. Put yourself under the plumbline of the Sermon on the Mount. Jump in.

So I did—and this is it. A journey of exploration, a risky and dangerous journey, demanding honest answers. Join me on the journey. It won't be as smooth as the 125 high speed rail trip from Doncaster to Kings Cross, but it won't, I hope, be dull, uninteresting or flat, either.

Let us sit and listen to Jesus as he spells out what the good life is all about. Is it enough to 'live by the Book'? Is it possible? What happens if we don't? What happens if we do?

Incidentally, if you want to find the Sermon on the Mount in the Bible, it is in Matthew's Gospel, chapters 5 to 7.

Introduction
to the Revised Edition

Reading through this book fourteen years after I wrote it has been like attempting one of those familiar puzzles which give two seemingly identical pictures with the challenge 'Spot the Difference'. Sometimes the differences are very obvious, other times quite subtle. For me it has been looking at the picture of life as I saw and experienced it in the mid-1980s and now, as I approach the new millennium, that awesome, magical, frightening and exciting prospect. Could any other digit-change cause such varying emotions and diverse opinions, I wonder? With all that in mind, have I changed very much in the last fourteen years, in my beliefs and hopes? Am I as certain as I was of the unchanging security that is to be had through faith in Jesus Christ; of the assurance and demands of the Word of God? Do I feel that in a world of rapid changes 'circumstances alter cases', or is 'living by the Book' still the blueprint for today, and for the twenty-first century?

Take the title of the book, *Living by the Book—a personal journey through the Sermon on the Mount*. That remains the same. Originally published by Triangle Books, I am delighted that it now appears again through the Bible Reading Fellowship, with a very different sort of cover and format, which we hope will attract new readers. I am the same person—or am I? I am fourteen years older, and surely I have changed and developed during that time? I hope I have been open to new insights and developments during the years. I have experienced many changes in my own life and situation. My husband is now retired, 'the children' have grown up and become established in their own lives and careers and, while not retired myself, I could be if I chose to be, for I have attained the age of 'senior citizen' and enjoy all the benefits available. In 1987 I was ordained deacon and, in 1994, priest, which has been a glorious bonus, and for which I thank God every day. We still live in the same house, in the same village. I work in the same parish, that of St James, Selby, and still enjoy writing and broadcasting. I still find enjoyment in the same hobbies, riding my bicycle, travel, music, meeting people. I still make some of the same mistakes, am prone to the same weaknesses, and retain the same sense of humour, which is a blessing to me, even though it may not always be to other people! I still travel frequently by train, especially on that Doncaster to Kings Cross route. Nowadays the journey takes a few minutes less—on a good day—than in the 1980s. The trains and their staff have a smart new livery and title, now Great North Eastern Railway, but it is more difficult to sleep, talk or read on the trains due to the incessant clatter of laptop computers and the shrill ringing of mobile phones. However, time after time, as conversations are struck up, the questions are still the same concerning the purpose of life and how to live it, with the frequent observation, 'If everybody lived by the Sermon on the Mount the world would be a better place', and I am challenged afresh by that word 'everybody', knowing full well that it means this body as well as all the others. As I have re-read my own book, *Living by the Book*, and reflected on the past years, I am more firmly convinced than ever that it is by listening to the One who preached that Sermon on the Mount, by responding to him personally and wholeheartedly and resolving by his grace and power to follow him, that life can and will be different. Life can be a positive, joyful adventure, and whatever happens, the future, tomorrow, next month, the next millennium, will hold no fears, only the 'sure and certain hope' of a glorious eternity with God.

In 1985 I concluded my exploration of the Sermon on the Mount with these words: 'To hear is not enough. To agree is insufficient. Jesus calls for immediate action and for our wholehearted obedience—and there is no substitute for either.' I repeat that now; for me, it says it all. But you have to make up your own mind, come to your own conclusions, follow your own path. Only you can do that. I wish you well on your journey of exploration, and pray you will discover the way, the truth and the life, and make it your own.

Margaret Cundiff

Sit down — and listen!

Matthew 5:1—2

By anyone's standards they were a strange, ill-assorted bunch of men. The two sets of brothers, Peter and Andrew, James and John, were in the same line of business—fishing; but when you'd said that you had said all, for they were entirely different in temperament. Then there was Philip, the quiet one, and his friend, rather a sceptic, called Bartholomew. Thomas, who always seemed to look at the dark side of things, and Matthew—well, he'd been in a very shady line before joining up with them, a tax collector, not the most popular with the local folk. There were three who seemed to be very much in the 'second eleven', James, Simon and Judas. And then the bright one of the bunch, the other Judas. He seemed to be in charge of the cash, quite an ambitious sort of chap.

Twelve men, so different in background, outlook and ability. The lively and the quiet, the enthusiasts and the pessimists, the thinkers and the doers, the cautious and the impetuous. None of them the sort to set the world on fire, not likely to make much impact on society, but for some reason attracted to the wandering preacher, Jesus—and he must have had something, because they had all dropped what they were doing, given up their jobs, and gone with him. He, really, was all they had in common. He was their leader, their friend, and he understood them, seemed to be able to meet them each on their own wavelength, and somehow enabled them to get along together, although at times there were flare-ups; but he seemed to be able to sort it all out with a word, or by just looking at them. Strange, really.

Why had they given up everything to follow him? They must have felt that their lives were incomplete, that there were questions to which no one could give a satisfactory answer. They had met him and they knew, although they could not have explained it, that he held the answer, that he *was* the answer, and that they just had to go with him.

As Jesus looked at them, what did he see in them? He saw what no one else could see, that here were men who would change the world, because through him they would become changed men. Shadows lay across the path of all of them; following him would cost everything they had. And across one lay a darker and deeper shadow, the shadow of total despair. The one who held the purse strings so tightly would die on the end of a rope, the knot pulled tight by his own hand, because he would in the end sell Jesus for a few jingling pieces of silver. Yes, a purse was very important to Judas—and yet as Jesus looked at him he loved him as much as any of the others, for after all, in one way or another, before their days of travelling together were done, they would all let him down.

Twelve men—what chance had they, these ordinary working men? After all, look at history, at the great and famous, the mighty leaders, the superb organizers, the intellectual giants, the convincing orators, the rising stars, the fallen idols, the forgotten 'unforgettables'—how could it be that they would fail and this bunch of 'common men' would be known for ever? The One who looked at them saw what others failed to see. That One still holds the answer, and still offers it freely. What he says is, 'Listen, if you have ears!'

What Jesus had to say, then, to those who would listen, was so extraordinary it took their breath away. In fact it turned many right away, for what he had to say didn't make sense, was quite unworkable. No one could run their lives on the lines he laid down and make any sort of success of them. His way was a way of disaster—or was it? Some were willing to take the chance, whose ears heard something more than mere words. They heard him on that quiet hillside, they took in what he was saying, and then went and lived out what he had taught them, and life changed completely.

It was turned upside-down—or right-side-up, depending on which angle you viewed it from!

Today, two thousand years after Jesus gathered his friends round him and taught them about a new way of life, a new kingdom—the kingdom of God—we hear the same words. We hear them read out in church on Sunday mornings as we sit down for our weekly dose of Christianity with like-minded friends, and we nod approvingly when the vicar says, 'This is the word of the Lord.' We glance at those words in our leather-bound Bible (or brightly coloured paperback edition) and think, 'Ah, if only people believed that today.'

But what do we do when the car won't start, the kids are at each other's throats, the man next door is a pain in the neck, and we arrive at work to find there has been a break-in and what we have worked so hard for is all ruined? What about when the plea for help comes just as we were going to put our feet up, or when suddenly the bottom drops out of our world as we read that letter, or hear what that solemn-faced doctor has to tell us as he calls us into his office at the hospital—when you look out at the world which seems just varying shades of black and grey, and you think, 'What's the point?' What has 'This is the word of the Lord' to do with all this?

Could it be that it has everything to do with it? Could what Jesus said to those folk sitting on the hillside two thousand years ago have anything to say to you and me? After all, two thousand years ago life was different, people were different. Were they? Does human nature change? Do fundamental principles change? Does Jesus change? For doesn't the Bible say of him, 'Jesus Christ is the same, yesterday, today and forever'? And maybe he is still saying to us, 'Listen—if you have ears.'

Jesus saw the crowds and went up a hill, where he sat down. His disciples gathered round him, and he began to teach them.

Happiness is...

Matthew 5:3—12

Do you remember the song, 'I want to be happy...'? Or maybe you have only heard it on one of those 'yesterday' programmes, for it's very much a yesterday song—and yet what it says is very much the song of any day. It is the song we all sing in one way or another, because we all want to be happy, of course we do! I want to be happy, I want my family to be happy, I want my friends to be happy, I want everybody to be happy—unless it costs me.

But how can I be happy, really happy? Life doesn't depend on me. I'm not in control of my world. I can't regulate it to suit me. I can't even guarantee my own health—the common cold which makes me so miserable is still without a cure; so if I can't even escape the common cold, I can't escape the chills and ills of modern life. The value of the pound goes up and down like a seesaw, and my feelings likewise. I am totally dependent on what happens to me for whether I will be happy or not. I can't demand happiness, although I would like to. I can't earn it, beg, borrow or steal it, because I only have to read the daily newspaper to see what happens to people who think they can. I just want to be happy, and if there is a way, I'd be a fool not to take it. How was it the song went? 'I want to be happy, and I can't be happy, till I've made you happy too...'

Jesus said it was possible to be happy right now. He said there are happy people around who have discovered the secret, and he spelled it out as he talked to people on the hillside. He seemed to have a strange understanding of what happiness is, though, for he said:

Happy are those who know they are spiritually poor;
the Kingdom of heaven belongs to them!
Happy are those who mourn;
God will comfort them!
Happy are those who are humble;
they will receive what God has promised!
Happy are those whose greatest desire is to do what God requires;
God will satisfy them fully!
Happy are those who are merciful to others;
God will be merciful to them!
Happy are the pure in heart;
they will see God!
Happy are those who work for peace;
God will call them his children!
Happy are those who are persecuted
because they do what God requires;
the Kingdom of heaven belongs to them!
Happy are you when people insult you and persecute you and tell all
kinds of evil lies against you because you are my followers.

What sort of happiness is that?

Spiritually poor? Wouldn't it be better to be spiritually rich? I suppose what he was getting at was knowing you are in need of help, because it is only as you recognize your need that you will begin to try to find help. All those people who shouted for help to Jesus, they knew their need all right, and knew who would help them. And he always helped them and gave them a new start in life, whether it was in their relationships, their health, their fear, or their failures. Most of all, he gave them a relationship with God that they had not known was possible. And it was quite simple, really. He gave them himself. They did become very happy people, and it did not depend on what happened to them, but it was because of something that happened *in* them; and the great thing was, it went on happening. As long as they needed him, and recognized that they needed him, he was there.

Yes, my happiest moments have often come through knowing I

needed help, and telling him I did, and it has been worth going through that to know more of him. When I have felt so lost because I know I have made such a mess of things, when I have felt desperately sorry for something I have done, I have realized I have lost something good in my life. It has been like mourning, like being bereaved, and I have cried and felt, 'If only I could have another chance.' And he has come alongside, given me a new start, wiped my tears away, and put me on my feet again. In that I have experienced happiness of a quality that I have not ever known before.

Jesus says, 'Happy are the humble.' A friend of mine laughingly said to me one day, 'I suppose your next book will be called *Humility and how I overcame it!*' I laughed too, but afterwards when I thought about it I realized that he had been gently reminding me of something very important. As things go well with us, we get so self-sufficient that we think we can manage our lives perfectly well ourselves, and we get an inflated idea of our own importance. Then we start talking about our rights—and insisting we get them! We begin to feel discontented with what we have got, and decide that 'the grass is greener on the other side of the fence'. And we may not realize it, but we begin to make ourselves miserable—and others.

A long time ago I heard a story about a monkey who came across a big jar of nuts. He put his fist in and took a large handful. Lovely nuts, just what he wanted—but the trouble was, he couldn't get his fist out, and he couldn't get those nuts out. So there he stayed with his fist in the jar, and eventually he was caught by the hunters and that was the end of him.

Stupid monkey, he could have just taken one or two nuts, enjoyed them, and gone away home. Instead, he wanted the lot, and got nothing at all, except captivity. But that is nothing really to do with humility, or being content with what we have. Only a monkey would be silly enough to think he could grab everything and get away with it, and we are not like that—are we?

When a couple of the friends of Jesus started fighting about who would be the greatest, Jesus gently chided them and said, 'Whoever wants to be first must place himself last of all, and be the servant of all.' But with the service comes the assurance that God keeps his promise, and that promise is of his kingdom— worth more than a jar of nuts, or an earthly empire, isn't it?

Jesus said that we are happy when we want to do what God requires. What does God require, though? The prophet Micah answered that question in the eighth century BC, and it still holds good for us today: 'What he requires of us is this: to do what is just, to show constant love, and to live in humble fellowship with our God' (Micah 6:8).

To do what is right, to love others at all times, not just some of the time; and, yes, that word 'humble' again. Seeing ourselves as we are—before God. Seeing others as they are—before God. When we do this we shall have a totally different attitude to them and to ourselves. I remember my old vicar, when I was a teenager, saying to me as I grumbled about someone, 'If he had been the only person in the world, Jesus would still have gone to the cross—for him. If you had been the only person in the world, Jesus would still have gone to the cross—for you. Doesn't that put you and him in a special relationship?' I had to admit that it did!

To see other people as important, lovable, having dignity; that should make a difference to the way we behave towards them. It is not just a matter of seeing ourselves as other see us, but of seeing others as God sees them. That means we will allow them to be themselves, and at the same time show them we love them, even when it costs us a great deal more than we want to pay! 'You've got to make allowances for people,' I was told one day when I was getting very cross about someone who had caused me a lot of trouble. 'How much allowance do you expect me to make?' I muttered. The answer came back quietly, 'As much as Jesus makes for you.' End of conversation!

The man who well and truly put me in my place that day was one of God's peacemakers. We often think of a 'peacemaker' as someone who works in the corridors of power, who has a position of influence in the government, who jets about the world speaking at this conference or that; or alternatively as someone who sits down outside an airbase. Perhaps the peacemakers Jesus meant include the ordinary person who quietly brings peace into individual situations, takes the heat out of an argument, risks being misunderstood or thumped by the one he is trying to help. Am I prepared to be that sort of a peacemaker—prepared to take the knocks in the cause of peace? Am I willing to be persecuted, laughed at, ignored, taken advantage of, because I stand out for the things I believe are right, like the prophet said—justice, love and humility? It is hard, very hard, and I win a few, lose a few; but if I want to be happy, it's the only way!

I don't want to be made a fool of. I want to hit back, to meet insult with insult, blow with blow. I want sympathy. I want everyone to know how hard-done-to I am. I want to sulk and snarl and... I want to know the secret of happiness, and I won't find it that way, but only by God's way.

When I was a child, I enjoyed learning little rhymes, and I used to trot them out as my party pieces. One went like this:

> *Two men looked out from prison bars,*
> *One saw mud, the other stars.*

God shows me the stars, the heavens, the future with him. He shows me the way of happiness; and it's not by looking at mud, or by throwing it, but by getting a vision of himself in Jesus, of his way of looking at things.

'I want to be happy, and I can't be happy till I make you happy too...' I won't be happy until I make happiness available for others; until I make God happy—that's quite a thought, isn't it? I am capable of giving God happiness, by 'living by the book'—his Book. And I know this—it's the only sure recipe for happiness. So it must be worth following, don't you think?

What flavour are you?

Matthew 5:13

'Chaps like him are the salt of the earth—where would we be without them?' My attention was directed to a small man in the corner who was busily engaged in putting up trestle tables in readiness for the Spring Fayre. My companion was a local minister, and I'd gone along to see how the preparations were progressing, as I wanted to include some comments in the Sunday morning Breakfast Show. I knew what he meant, of course. The salt of the earth—the sort of people you can rely on, who get on with the job, who are prepared to put themselves out for others, whose lives show goodness, faith, reliability, love. They don't make a song and dance about what they do, but you know what they stand for, what they believe in, and they can be trusted a hundred per cent. They would be very surprised to hear themselves described as such; they just consider they are living as they should, getting on with what Jesus said: 'Love God, love your neighbour.'

The salt of the earth—an ordinary, everyday expression, describing good folk. Do you know who first said it? Jesus did, as he talked to his friends on the hillside. Can you imagine him looking at his friends, that varied bunch of men, very ordinary men really, with nothing special about them, apart from their determination to do what was right, and follow it out. As Jesus looked at them, his inner circle, he would see the wider circle also, those people clustered round, pushing in, straining their ears, wanting to know what he had to say. Jesus was teaching his disciples, yes, but not in a classroom situation. There were no tickets for admittance, no 'ivory towers' here. Anyone could hear what he had to say. Much of what he was saying was directed to his close friends, those who had given up everything to follow him. A lot was to those who wanted to know more about the way of life they had chosen to share with him; and some was to those who tried to trick him, trip him up, play games with him. What Jesus had to say was for those who had ears to hear; some would hear nothing, some a little. And for others? It would be a shattering experience; they could not just hear and listen, it demanded their immediate action.

There is an expression, 'If the cap fits, wear it!' Jesus didn't say it quite like that, but I have a feeling that is what he often meant. As he looked at his friends, those who hung on his words, he knew those who were 'the salt of the earth'. Oh yes, to the casual eye they would all have looked very much the same; it was well before the days of the High Street trendy outfitters, the wide range of clothes shops—so the fashion trade hadn't yet taken off! Yet some people were different, and would be called to be different, to indeed be 'salt'.

But what sort of a difference? There were no 'I love Jesus' badges to be had, but then what you are matters more than what you claim. It is easy to dress up in 'religious' clothes, to say the right words, to be seen with the right people; but what matters is the real you inside. Many claimed to follow Jesus and to be his friends; not all were. Jesus was saying, 'If you are claiming to be my friend, if you accept as true what I am telling you, then you have a job to do, and that is to be salt—salt for all mankind.'

Just think about salt, what effect it has. I know the difference it can make, as I found some time ago when I had prepared a special meal for my family. It looked marvellous on the plates. I stood back and admired my hard work in the kitchen, even heard the applause in my mind as I carried the dishes in and set them on the table. At lightning speed the food went from the plates into those smiling open mouths... and the expressions changed! 'Ugh, there's no taste in this... you've forgotten the salt, Mum!' Yes, it did look so attractive set out on the plates. I had used the very best ingredients, and followed the recipe very carefully, but as they said, I'd forgotten the salt; and that made all the difference. Just that small measure of salt.

'Put some on now,' I urged, and they did, but it didn't solve the problem. It needed to have been in there right from the beginning. Being put on afterwards was not the same.

Jesus said we are to be 'like salt for all mankind' that is you and me, and all of us who claim to be following his way. Adding flavour and taste, giving pleasure, bringing out the best. Well, we know that, don't we? The trouble is, we like to remain nice and cosy in our airtight, shrinkwrapped, brightly coloured, hygienic packet. It's so comfortable sitting on the shelf with all the other grains of salt, undisturbed. Who wants to get mixed up with all those strange people out there in the world? No, better to stay in the packet—labelled 'church', 'group' or 'fellowship'.

Mind you, sometimes we hear the shouts for help, the 'Ugh, there's no taste in life', see the signs of sheer boredom with what is being dished up out there, and we do a quick once-over, a sort of rescue effort at the last minute. But it doesn't work; we needed to have been there from the start. Like when that new baby came along and things were tough for the people across the road, when the husband was out of work. Like when the old fellow was in hospital and no one went to see him and he just pined away. Like when the youth club folded up because no one would help with the youngsters. When there had to be a cutback of the 'meals on wheels' service because of the lack of volunteers. When the local sex shop flourished because no one objected to it being so near the school, so it was obviously all right, they said.

'You are like salt for all mankind.' Are you? Am I? Of course, salt is used for so many purposes. It is vital for life itself. Did you know that the Romans used to be paid partly in salt? It was a valuable currency. That's where we got the expression 'not worth his salt' from!

Salt can be used for healing. Salt can be used for preserving. Salt can be used to stop us falling—a well-known remedy on an icy path! One winter when we had a big freeze-up, a friend of mine went outside and slipped on the ice and lay there, unable to get up. His wife tried to lift him and was unable to do so because of the slippery surface. Then, like the wise woman she is, she went inside and got the salt and scattered it all around him. In minutes it had done its work, she was able to get a firm hold and raise her husband up from his icy prison. They had cause to be thankful for the salt.

Salt isn't pretty. It has no smell, no exciting feel to it. When it is doing its job we take it for granted. It's only when it is missing that we recognize its worth.

Jesus said this about our work as salt:

You are like salt for all mankind. But if salt loses its saltiness,
there is no way to make it salty again. It has become worthless,
so it is thrown out and people trample on it.

I don't like being taken for granted, being thought of as 'ordinary'. Sometimes I get very cross when I feel I am being used. But if Jesus says I am to be salt, then he will also give me the grace to be so!

Lord—save me from being insipid and worthless. Help me to bring
a taste of you into the lives around me. For your sake. Amen.

Get switched on

Matthew 5:14—16

When I think about the people Jesus was talking to in the Sermon on the Mount, such very ordinary people, described as 'the common people'—those we would call 'the man and woman in the street'—it takes my breath away to hear them described as 'light for the whole world'. It sounds like gross exaggeration! Light for the whole world? A world dominated by the rich, the powerful, the strong. A world very alien to the ideals of the travelling preacher, Jesus. It was a strange thing to say to people who were under foreign occupation, who were in danger of obliteration should they stand out. When you were under a foreign power, then as now, the wisest thing to do was to keep quiet and merge into the scenery. That way you might survive. People who tried to light up the scene with new ideas soon got blown out.

Anyway, what sort of light had these 'common people' got? Uneducated, used only to their village life, they wouldn't stand a chance in any argument; they would be made a laughing stock of, and probably given a good hiding for their trouble.

In his Gospel account, John describes Jesus as 'the Word' and says of him, 'The Word was the source of life, and this life brought light to mankind. The light shines in the darkness, and the darkness has never put it out' (John 1:4, 5). Jesus used this symbol of light many times, saying, 'I am the light of the world. Whoever follows me will have the light of life and will never walk in darkness' (John 8:12). He did not say, 'Whoever follows me and goes to theological college', or 'Whoever follows me and has a high

IQ', or even, 'Whoever follows me and has attained the age of twenty-one'. He just said, '*Whoever* follows me will have the light of life'.

Are you a follower of Jesus? Do you belong to him? Are you seeking by his help to do what he says? Then you have the light of life; you are a light for the whole world—yes, you! You cannot hide away, live a quiet life, opt out. You are going to have to stand out as a light, even though sometimes you will feel like a sore thumb. Just like switching on the light in the living-room, you have got to be switched on, and to provide the light that is needed for anyone and everyone.

That idea frightens me. If I stand out, I am likely to get shot down, criticized, or shown up. Anyway, how dare I set myself up as a light for anyone? There are enough murky corners in my own life, plenty of dark areas which do not bear inspection. So what am I to do?

I remember one dark night driving along into Selby, my headlights full on, but I was hardly able to see a thing. I stopped the car to check the lights, because I was sure something was wrong with them; the bulbs must have failed. What I found was that the lights were perfectly all right—there was nothing wrong with the power or the bulbs—but the glass was filthy, covered in dirt and mud from previous journeys, and I had never bothered to clean it. The light was shining all right, but could not get through the dirt and muck. I got a cloth out of my boot, wiped the glass, got back in the car, and the road ahead lit up as if by magic. The problem had been caused through my own silly fault, of course! I had been just too lazy to clean the car, and had ignored the common-sense rule of day-to-day care.

It reminded me of a friend who worked in India for many years in the 'eye camps'. She went round the villages with a medical team who were able to carry out operations and give sight back to many who otherwise would have been blind; they also provided glasses to enable those with poor sight to see properly. One old fellow had cataracts removed and was overjoyed at having his eyesight again. He was given glasses to wear, and so made 'as good as new'.

A couple of years later, my friend again visited his village and found him huddled in a corner, still wearing his glasses, but unable to see; he was quite blind, or so he thought. She took away his glasses, cleaned off all the filth of two years and put them on him again. To his delight he could see! He had not realized that glasses had to be cleaned.

Could anyone be quite so stupid? I reckon they could; after all, I was, with my own car headlights. My blindness was due to laziness, the old man's to ignorance.

Jesus says that if we follow him we will have the light of life. That is absolutely true. He is 'the light of the world'—your light, my light; but it is so easy for us to obscure his light from shining. A modern version of the Prayer Book general confession puts it this way: 'Almighty God, our heavenly Father, we have sinned against you and our fellow men, in thought and word and deed, in the evil we have done, and in the good we have not done, through ignorance, through weakness, through our own deliberate fault...' Yes, that is what stops the light from shining—ignorance, weakness, and our own deliberate fault.

What we need to do is allow Jesus to clean us up, so that his light can shine through. His light is desperately needed; we have it, we must show it. We are to be examples, not so that people will say how marvellous we are, but so that they will see the light of Jesus in us, and will be able to praise God, because they have caught a glimpse of him.

God said, 'Let there be light,' and there was light. There is light, God's light, and the darkness will never put it out; but we can blur that light, we can coat it with dirt. It's a sobering thought, isn't it, that it's up to us how much light gets through. We have an awesome responsibility, and we also have a wonderful privilege. One day we will be called to account for our 'light-bearing'. One day we will stand in the full glare of God's light—and from that there is no escape.

Those people sitting on the hillside were just like you and me, a crowd of ordinary folk, with nothing very distinguished about them, the 'man and woman in the street'. The journey they had made to listen to Jesus was probably the longest they had ever made, and they would return to their very ordinary, everyday life; except for a handful of men whose names would be known for ever, because they lived out their lives in his light, the light we also are called to reflect in the darkness and gloom of our day.

You are like light for the whole world. A city built on a hill cannot be hidden. No one lights a lamp and puts it under a bowl; instead he puts it on the lampstand, where it gives light for everyone in the house. In the same way your light must shine before people, so that they will see the good things you do and praise your Father in heaven.

On the road home

Matthew 5:17—20

One of the great joys of living in North Yorkshire is that the city of York is just up the road—about half an hour's journey. It could be said that 'all roads lead to York'—the Rome of our day! Although I travel into the city of York frequently, it has never become a chore, a bore or mere duty, even when I am going for the most mundane reason, for a committee meeting, for shopping, or to fetch someone from the railway station. I always have a sense of excitement, of joy. In fact, each trip is a small pilgrimage.

This is not because York is a most beautiful city, that there are treasures to be explored, that it is steeped in history, that there are always new exhibitions to enjoy, the river trips are delightful, the shops are superb and the cakes delicious; but because the centre of York is the Minster. I can see the Minster as I drive along the road, and like a magnet it beckons me, welcomes me, and I respond with love.

York Minster is a 'must' for every visitor, and every day of the year, whatever the weather, people stream into it, guidebooks in hand, discovering for themselves the glories of the ancient church, and hopefully coming into contact not only with a building, with history, but with God; because it is not a museum or a historic monument, but the house of God, alive and active. Worship is continually being offered, both in the regular services which are held each day, and as individuals and groups join in prayer and praise.

It is interesting, and often amusing, to see the crocodiles of trippers and tourists heading towards the Minster—earnest-looking Americans with scholarly guides, cheerful members of clubs and organizations on a day's outing; and the chattering school parties, with the anxious-looking teachers trying to keep their youthful charges in order, steering them in the right direction as various youngsters try to escape to the river or climb the city walls or go into the cafés. I often feel sorry for the children; after all, they are on a day out, and rivers, walls and snack bars are much more exciting than visiting churches!

Often as I look at reluctant children being shepherded into the Minster, I think of Moses and his flock. What a job he had, leading the people of God, that unruly rabble, out of slavery in Egypt, to the freedom of the promised land! In charge of a complaining, weak and often downright disobedient people, and with whip and carrot keeping them together on the journey, holding before them the vision of what it meant to be God's people, and to be travelling in his direction.

You could say Moses hadn't an earthly chance of making it. The odds were stacked against him; except that he held the ace card—God was with him, God held him, and provided all that was needed on the journey. To make the journey, the people needed food and water; God provided them. They needed protection; God provided it. They needed directions; God provided them. They needed the will and the obedience—that was their responsibility! And they came unstuck many, many times, but God still picked them up, still provided for them, and still pointed them in the right direction.

God gave his people what they most needed, which was more than food or clothing or power; it was a set of rules to live by—rules which gave them freedom and protection, so that they would know where they were, with God and with each other.

Lord Blanch, former Archbishop of York, in his book *Trumpet in the Morning*, says this:

> *The picture is not so much of a stern judge handing down judgments and imposing fearful penalties, as of a father teaching his child how to walk and what to eat and how to avoid danger. Introducing him to new truths, opening his eyes to the stately ordering of the universe.*

The Ten Commandments are universally known. They are accepted as the standards for all human behaviour. Not just for a wandering people in the wilderness, pressing on towards their promised land, but for men and women who struggle through the wilderness of life today, who have a longing to reach the better land, who have a vision of what might be, could be, should be, will be; who, whether they realize it or not, are travelling to meet with God. He is the beginning and the end, the 'Alpha and Omega', the start and the arrival point.

So we have the God-given laws by which to travel in company with him and with each other. It should be quite simple. After all, here they are, written down plainly so that anyone can understand. But they are meant to be written not just on tablets of stone, or in bold letters on a page, but on the heart—and there's the snag! For as Jeremiah wrote: 'Who can understand the human heart? There is nothing else so deceitful' (Jeremiah 17:9). So it was not long before the human heart got to work on the commandments of God and began to twist them, bend them, tighten them, working on them to mould them to suit. So other commandments which had been intended as the plumb-line against which all human action was to be measured became a piece of string to be cut and used as required, to parcel up man-made ideas, weaknesses, prejudices, demands and excuses.

Jesus came to unwrap those parcels, untangle the string, and draw out again the plumb-line and hold it before the people. As Moses constantly drew the people's attention back to God's commandments, so Jesus draws the attention of his hearers to what was at the heart of them.

Jesus was the teacher *par excellence*. He knew exactly what was going on in the heads and hearts of those who sat so attentively before him. He knew that in him they saw an easy way of life, devoid of rules and regulations. All their lives they had been tied down by the obligations of the Law, and by petty regulations made by those who thought they were the guardians of the Law. Now here was someone who was above all that, who could show a way of freedom.

Do not think that I have come to do away with the Law of
Moses and the teachings of the prophets. I have not come to do

away with them, but to make their teachings come true.
Remember that as long as heaven and earth last, not the least
point nor the smallest detail of the Law will be done away
with—not until the end of all things. So then, whoever disobeys
even the least important of the commandments and teaches
others to do the same, will be least in the Kingdom of heaven.
On the other hand, whoever obeys the Law and teaches others to
do the same, will be great in the Kingdom of heaven. I tell you,
then, that you will be able to enter the Kingdom of heaven only if
you are more faithful than the teachers of the Law and the
Pharisees in doing what God requires.

The Law of Moses and the teaching of the prophets—the God-given way that made for reverence and respect for God and one's fellow human beings. These were for all time the standards set, and Jesus had come to show the way to attain them. Not to say, 'These are too hard for you, beyond your capability, forget them,' but to show men and women the way of freedom within them. The scribes and Pharisees had thought the way was by even more rules and regulations as ladders to reach the seemingly unobtainable, and instead had created a mesh which entangled the people; no wonder the ordinary people had lost heart.

Jesus came to make 'the Law and the prophets' not only possible, but actual, but with an additional law—the law of love. Augustine said, many years after he had come through a wild youth of disobedience and rebellion against parents, society and God, into faith, that the Christian way of life was quite a simple matter. It could be summed up completely in one small sentence: 'Love God, and do what you like.' And of course, the secret lies in the way round it was put. Not 'Do what you like, and love God', but 'Love God, and do what you like.'

Jesus says we are to obey the Law and teach others to do the same. Notice the order! Obey it yourself first, says Jesus, then teach it to others. It is so easy to say, 'Do as I say, and not as I do.' The hard bit is being obedient ourselves first, *then* teaching other people. We cannot take anyone further than we ourselves have gone. We cannot dictate to others. But we can show the truth of what we are saying by what we are.

Jesus could speak as strongly as he did because he was obedient; obedient to death. That didn't mean he had no will or mind of his own—of course he had, and what he would have chosen to do was not always the way it had to be. In fact, he asked that his way might be easier. In the garden of Gethsemane he prayed, 'My Father, if it is possible, take this cup of suffering from me! Yet not what I want, but what you want' (Matthew 26:39). Obedience is not easy, not when everything within us strains to go in the other direction; and Jesus knew all about that, but still could say, 'Yet not my will...'

Sinless perfection? Yes, it was for Jesus. But for me? For you? Impossible! But Jesus was not talking about the dotting of 'i's and crossing of 't's. He meant something far bigger than that. He was talking about doing what God requires.

It is not a matter of having a list of 'things I must do', and giving ourselves a gold star at the end for having crossed through all the list, but of being in a right relationship with other people and with God. Not merely of being 'Captain Sensible', making sure we are all right, keeping our noses clean, but of loving others and loving God. I remember doing something some years ago which cost me a great deal. It was not the most sensible thing to do, I suppose, and I got quite a lot of stick from my friends about it. They said, 'You can't let your heart rule your head.' Maybe they were right at the time, but I do not think we can live life with our heads ruling all the time. I believe Jesus says that our hearts must rule our heads, even if it costs us. I once read in the local paper of a young couple who had sold up their home and gone out to a difficult part of the world to try to help people who lived in absolute squalor. They went out under no official society, with no real backing except the prayers and promises of a few friends. They went because they said God had called them to do it. My initial feeling was, 'They must be off their heads. If they want to serve God, why not do it through a missionary society, or an agency here in this country? How are they going to manage? What will they do if they are ill? What about when children come along? How can they afford to live on faith?'

Jesus has something to say about those questions a bit later on in his Sermon on the Mount. I cannot answer for other people, but I must answer to him for myself, for Jesus speaks to each of us personally. He does not say 'they', but 'you'. It will not work to throw up other people's problems, other situations. Jesus looks us each straight in the eye and says, 'I tell you...' I want to avert my eyes. I don't want to meet his gaze, but I must. I cannot escape from the searching, searing, burning eyes of Jesus. Yet as I timidly look at him, I see in those eyes love and compassion. He is not looking at me through rose-coloured spectacles but seeing me as I am, as I really am. He looks at my heart, my intentions, my desires. He holds his hand out and says, 'You can do it if you let me do it with you.'

It is only as I grasp that hand by faith, as I allow him to teach me the way to go, that I can begin to teach others.

Murder — he says

Matthew 5:21—26

The most precious and personal thing we each possess is the gift of our life. Anyone who takes another's life is guilty of breaking the commandment of God: 'Do not commit murder.' It has no 'ifs' or 'buts'. Murder is the most deadly of all sins, for it is irreversible. Once it has been committed, it has been committed, and nothing can alter that fact. All the tears, apologies, offerings cannot alter the fact once it has happened. There is no putting the clock back, no way of 'making up'.

So what did the people think as Jesus stood up and said, 'You have heard that people were told in the past, "Do not commit murder; anyone who does will be brought to trial"'? I imagine they thought, 'Quite right, so they should be. But why tell us? After all, we haven't killed anyone, we are in the clear. It's not us he should be telling, it's those murdering bandits and robbers who roam the countryside; the evil men in the pay of a foreign oppressor who put to death those who dare lift up their voice or hand against them; and those who cannot control their passion and anger and who kill for vengeance—it is they who have broken God's holy law.'

We read our newspapers, watch television, listen to the radio, with their daily parade of murders with all the sordid details. The massacres, the result of war and conflict. Premeditated murders, planned and executed in cold blood. Then the crimes of passion, committed on the spur of the moment, the accidents—'I didn't mean to do it!'—and the murders that are done because of greed, hatred, fear and jealousy, and those carried out for reasons of revenge, political gain or ideological superiority. Why is there such an interest in murder trials, I wonder? Why do the crowds gather to see the accused brought into court, or leaving it, with a blanket over his or her head, hustled into a van and driven speedily away? Why is it that murder stories, both fact and fiction, are so avidly read, that the most horrific films containing brutal killings are deemed 'entertainment'? I sometimes have the feeling that if public executions were carried out again in this country, the crowds would flock to see them.

Is it, I wonder, because we like to feel self-righteous? After all, we wouldn't do such a thing as murder. So that means we are all right, it enhances our sense of goodness; we are safe and secure in our castle of contentment, viewing from the safety of our turrets the miserable sinners out there in the world. We can cast our stones down with the rest, with smug satisfaction.

If so, we need to take a deep breath before we hear what Jesus went on to say, because it is to us he says it. Right now. Ready, then? Here it is.

But now I tell you: whoever is angry with his brother will be brought to trial, whoever calls his brother 'You good-for-nothing!' will be brought before the Council, and whoever calls his brother a worthless fool will be in danger of going to the fire of hell. So if you are about to offer your gift to God at the altar and there you remember that your brother has something against you, leave your gift there in front of the altar, go at once and make peace with your brother, and then come back and offer your gift to God.

If someone brings a lawsuit against you and takes you to court, settle the dispute with him while there is time, before you get to court. Once you are there, he will hand you over to the judge, who will hand you over to the police, and you will be put in jail. There you will stay, I tell you, until you pay the last penny of your fine.

I imagine there was an uneasy silence as Jesus finished speaking those words, followed by an embarrassing averting of the eyes, and shuffling of feet, as the full impact of what he had said began to sink in. Memories of conversations, observations, condemnations. Perhaps of some things that had happened only minutes before as they jostled for a better position, and that 'stupid fool' in front had blocked their view, and the 'idiot' on their right had trodden on their toe. They had told him where to get off all right—or would have done if he hadn't been several inches taller or a stone heavier!—so they had given him a dirty look, and muttered under their breath. Surely Jesus couldn't really mean that being angry, calling someone a few choice names, or even feeling bad-tempered, was in the same league as murder? Then what was all that about remembering some little thing that had happened and having to go and sort it out before going to the temple? As long as you intended to say something next time you saw the person, that should be enough; and anyway, you had no lawsuit pending, so that didn't apply at all... And yet Jesus disturbed them. He seemed to have put his finger on some very sore points. It had all become a bit too close for comfort, for if Jesus meant what he had said, then there would have to be very radical changes—in fact Jesus was asking for the impossible, knowing human nature.

Yes, I'm sure the people around Jesus that day had cause to be anxious; and as the words come thundering across the page to us we also avert our eyes, shuffle our feet, go hot under the collar—but to no avail.

Some time ago I was sitting waiting for a friend when suddenly I felt a tap on my shoulder and there was someone I hadn't seen for ages. She sat down beside me and soon we were chattering away, happily catching up on news. 'What are you doing here?' she asked me. 'I'm waiting for John X,' I replied. Before I could say another word she jumped to her feet and, frowning, said, 'Then I'll be off. I don't want to meet him again; we are not on speaking terms. We had a row some time ago.' I was surprised. Neither of them seemed the sort to have rows, so it must have been something very serious. 'What about?' I queried. 'Oh, something and nothing, it doesn't really matter now...' She was already walking quickly away before I could ask her any more.

When John arrived, I told him what had happened. He shrugged his shoulders, coloured up slightly and muttered, 'Oh yes, I'd forgotten about that, it was just one of those things.' It was very evident that the matter was now closed—there was to be no further discussion!

'Just one of those things...' Yes, they happen to us all at times. Something is said or done, perhaps quite innocently, then words fly carelessly, tempers fray at the edges, we are caught on the raw, and we go on our way. It may have been a flaming row, or just a small misunderstanding, but it has never been resolved, and with the passing of time it has grown out of all proportion, like a festering sore, untreated, unhealed. The infection is passed on, too, by remarks made to other people, the snide comments and the bitter insinuations.

Now I wouldn't call that murder, would you? But Jesus says there's no difference in essence, so the penalty is as for murder, it's the death penalty. And that makes the shivers run down the spine, doesn't it? So maybe we should take notice of what Jesus is saying. And, thinking about it, isn't it true that when we are at outs with someone, we have deprived them of something very precious? When we harbour grudges and resentments we are killing off something very valuable, and when we attack the character of another we have assassinated their spirit. I remember another friend who was frequently verbally attacked. He confided, 'I can never say anything back in defence, because when he starts on me I just curl up and die inside.' He died the death over and over again as he was lashed by another's tongue, a murderous tongue. No wonder James in his epistle warns us of the dangers of the tongue: 'The tongue is like a fire. It is a world of wrong, occupying its place in our bodies and spreading evil through our whole being. It sets on fire the entire course of our existence with the fire that comes to it from hell itself' (James 3:6).

We are condemned out of our own mouths. How often too do we come to God in prayer, asking for forgiveness, for his help in our lives, his blessing, and at the same time being unwilling to forgive someone else? How many times do we come to the Holy Communion service and take into our hands the reminders of the broken body and the shed blood of Jesus Christ, and yet will not hold out those hands in forgiveness and friendship, in help and healing for others? How often, too, are those hands stained with bitterness, anger, envy and hate. Jesus says that before we can come, we must make our peace with our brother. Making peace is something he knows all about, for he is our peace. He didn't die on the cross so that there might be an uneasy ceasefire, a temporary lull in the action. He died so that we might be at peace with one another and with God. That means forgiving and forgetting, putting the past right away in the right way!

I like the story of the boy saying his prayers: 'Dear God, please forgive me, I've gone and done it again...' and the answer came, 'Done what, my son?' If God can forgive and forget, then I reckon we ought to, and do it quickly, because we may not get another chance.

What Jesus says so very clearly is that we must have our relationships right, and then our actions will be right. Stop before things get out of hand!

We all need pulling up sharp, to see ourselves as we really are. And if we will listen, will stop, will admit our fault, our sin and our responsibility, then there is hope, there is help.

If we say that we have no sin, we deceive ourselves, and there is no truth in us. But if we confess our sins to God, he will keep his promise and do what is right: he will forgive us our sins and purify us from all our wrongdoing (1 John 1:8, 9).

And that is a promise that will never be broken.

... and they lived happily ever after

Matthew 5:27—32

For the past two hours or so we had been in the magic land of pantomime. Against all odds, the poor boy had overcome evil, poverty and ignorance and had won the hand of the beautiful princess. Now, hand in hand, they took centre stage. Love had conquered all; as man and wife they would go off into their fairy-tale castle, and live happily ever after. We, the audience, sighed with pleasure, cheered with delight and, as the curtain fell, gathered up our coats and scarves, almost-empty boxes of chocolates, the half-asleep children, and pushed our way out into the cold, dark, real world. Every pantomime is predictable. We know, whatever the title, that the story will follow the same line: love always wins the day, and the last line will for ever be '...and they lived happily ever after'.

Sadly, we do not live in fairyland, pantomime time or the world of make-believe, where the good fairy has only to wave her magic wand and all is sweetness and light. We live in reality, where more than wishes wrapped in tinsel is needed to ensure that 'they live happily ever after'. We live in a society where one in three marriages ends in the divorce courts, where the daily papers churn out a diet of lust masquerading as love, of centre-page lovers standing amid the confetti of broken promises, torn relationships and wrecked lives.

It is no longer fashionable to speak of adultery; it is now a 'meaningful relationship', or a 'live-in situation'. Call it love, the world says, for the word will cover a multitude of sins; but God calls adultery sin, an offence against his creation, against his ordained plan for humanity. His express command was, 'Do not commit adultery'—short, sharp, and to the point; and the penalty for disobedience was to be death.

The people of Jesus' day knew the law and the penalty, and there was no shortage of those willing to carry out the sentence of stoning, ready to obey the letter of the law, with a self-righteousness as hard and sharp as the stones they hurled.

'Caught in the act'—we read of such a woman in John's Gospel, chapter 8, brought before Jesus by the teachers of the law and the Pharisees. They knew the law all right, they knew they were on safe ground by quoting the scriptures; but what had Jesus to say? No doubt they were eager to get on with the execution, but more eager to hear Jesus condemn himself before them, either by his denial of the Law of Moses, or by his complicity in the woman's death. He kept them waiting, not even looking at them; he let them go on questioning, until at last he spoke: 'Whichever one of you has committed no sin may throw the first stone at her.' Then he turned away from them, leaving the judge and jury to face the judgment of their own hearts. The law was in their hands, but the words of Jesus found their mark far more accurately than their stones would have hit the target standing before their eyes. They were right on target with their book of rules; Jesus was right on target with his question. We read that 'when they heard this, they all left, one by one, the older ones first'. They looked into their own hearts and saw what was there, and turned away, convicted by the evidence.

What of the woman standing there? What did she make of it all? She knew her guilt, she knew the penalty; what did she expect from Jesus? He could have cast those stones dropped by her embarrassed and convicted judges. He, who was without sin, could have carried out the sentence—he was within his rights—but all he did was ask where those who condemned her had gone... and he gave her back the life she had thought was over, a second chance. Not to pick up the threads of the old sinful life, but to make a new start, with his instruction, 'Go, but do not sin again.'

The commandments of God, the words of scripture, stand firm. Jesus made that point clear, as he said, ' I have not come to do away with them, but to make their teachings come true.' His was no soft option, but he made people see beyond the words to the spirit of them, always tempered by the law of love.

The commandments and words of scripture are the plumb-lines against which we measure ourselves; they are not missiles to be hurled against others. How often, though, they are taken up to be thrown at others, to be deadly weapons of destruction, to injure, maim and destroy, rather than to be the means of building up, strengthening and instructing. We use 'proof texts' to relieve ourselves of having to answer the hard questions. We hide behind them, shelving our own responsibility; we do not want to be forced to think for ourselves.

Human nature does not change. We still want a rule book by which to judge others rather than a guidebook to show us the way of life. Jesus was always being asked questions by those who wanted to put him on the spot. They laid their traps, oh, so cunningly and cleverly, and fell into them head first. Jesus has that very uncomfortable habit of taking us by the shoulders and turning us round to face our own questions, so that we, the judges, find ourselves in the dock.

So what did Jesus say about adultery? About the woman who was brought before him? About the famous figures who make the gossip columns, the man up the road who is 'having a bit on the side'? He said this:

> You have heard that it was said, 'Do not commit adultery.'
> But now I tell you: anyone who looks at a woman and wants to
> possess her is guilty of committing adultery with her in his
> heart. So if your right eye causes you to sin, take it out and
> throw it away! It is much better for you to lose a part of your
> body than to have your whole body thrown into hell. If your
> right hand causes you to sin, cut it off and throw it away! It is
> much better for you to lose one of your limbs than for your
> whole body to go to hell.

> It was also said, 'Anyone who divorces his wife must give her a
> written notice of divorce.' But now I tell you: if a man divorces

his wife, even though she has not been unfaithful, then he is
guilty of making her commit adultery if she marries again; and
the man who marries her commits adultery also.

Some time ago, I took part in a radio discussion on the subject of adultery, based on a magazine article entitled 'You don't have to take your clothes off to be unfaithful!' which, when you begin to think about it, is quite true! It was a very clever article, because as you read it and began to feel quite self-righteous, it suddenly turned on you and, instead of giving answers, posed very hard questions; and one of those questions was this: 'Does unfaithfulness start in the head or the bed?' Where do you draw the line? At what stage does adultery begin? Not in legal terms, but in moral terms. Not a matter of producing the hotel bill receipt for that double room in the name of Mr and Mrs Jones, but when did two people cross the line of friendship into the area marked 'adultery'? Is there a sliding scale, which can be pushed up and down according to the circumstances, or is there a point on the scale marked in red?

Our radio discussion on the subject was fascinating, and in one way it was 'You pays your money and takes your choice'—except for one thing. That red point on the scale was clearly marked for us, whatever we had to say, already marked out by Jesus: 'I tell you, anyone who looks at a woman and wants to possess her is guilty of committing adultery with her in his heart'—and for 'woman' also read 'man', and for 'his', 'her'. So now it is no longer an academic exercise but a human response. Do you plead guilty or not guilty? Yes, you, happily married mother of those two delightful youngsters. Yes, you, hardworking husband, pillar of the church. Yes, you, Chairman of the Council; yes, you, untiring fundraiser for the underprivileged... yes, you, both writer and reader of religious books! Guilty, or not guilty?

Like the would-be stone-throwers we read about in John's Gospel, we turn away, turn away convicted...

But the words of Jesus to the woman ring in our ears: 'Go, but do not sin again.' We are convicted, not to wallow in our own self-pity, but to take action, not against others but to do something about our own future. Recognize that it does start in the head, in the looking, in the wanting, and nip it in the bud.

Have you ever tried to nip something in the bud? The more you think about the thing that has to be nipped, the more attractive it becomes. You find yourself drawn to it like a moth to the flame—it becomes even more desirable, until it burns you up. It's like telling a child not to do something; the more you emphasize the 'thing', the more desirable it becomes! I can think of many things in my life that I have been told not to do, which I had never considered until told not to do them, and at that very moment they became the one thing I was most determined to do! I suppose we all secretly believe it is a devious plot to stop us enjoying ourselves and getting the most out of life. That's the take Eve fell for anyway, and look what happened to her.

Jesus says, 'Stop thinking about it and get rid of it altogether.' He paints the picture on a large canvas, talking about pulling out eyes and cutting off hands. What he is saying is, 'Stop looking in that direction, stop putting your hand out to take what is not yours. Don't kid yourself you can play with fire, because you can't.'

All right, shut your eyes, fold your arms… So what happens? The 'thing' is still there in your mind's eye, in your desire. Then use your eye, use your hand, in quite another direction. Be positive, not negative. The apostle Paul gives some good advice when writing to the Philippians: 'Fill your minds with those things that are good and that deserve praise: things that are true, noble, right, pure, lovely, and honourable' (Philippians 4:8).

What Jesus has to say, what Paul advises, is not airy-fairy idealism but down-to-earth common sense. Face up to the fact that we all play with fire, we all try to have our own scale of values which can be moved according to how we feel. Recognize that fact. Recognize that fuelling the fire of desire by looking at soft porn and calling it fun, or excusing the slap and tickle by calling it 'fellowship', is to be cut out. It does start in the head, and you get to the bed much quicker than you ever imagined! Most adultery starts as 'just a bit of fun', and Christians are not exempt, in fact are often blind to it because of the religious jargon they use to disguise what is sinful. Sin is terribly catching, far more infectious than measles, and sadly one person can be the ruination of a happy marriage, a united family, an entire fellowship—can ruin that which was beautiful and wholesome and good, can wreck years of Christian growth in a locality, can damage almost beyond repair the Christian witness in an area.

The psychologists advise sublimation. Jesus offers transformation, if we will see ourselves as we are, warts and all, and turn, not away in disgust and self pity, but to him in penitence and faith. His promise is abundant life, freed by his grace.

Promises, promises

Matthew 5:33—37

Scene one: the courtroom is crowded with court officials, police officers and legal representatives. The jury listens intently, while the steely-eyed, bewigged judge sits impassively taking note of all that is going on. The press are busily writing up their copy for the papers' deadlines, and the members of the public up in the gallery crane forward to see what is happening. The witness steps into the box, takes 'the book' in his right hand, and as instructed says, 'I swear by Almighty God that the evidence I shall give shall be the truth, the whole truth, and nothing but the truth.' With the taking of the oath, he and all those present recognize the solemnity of the occasion, for on the evidence that follows could rest the character and future of another person. The witness has promised to tell the truth, before God. That promise has given his words weight, and should it later be proved that he is not telling the truth, not honouring his promise, then he will be in very serious trouble indeed.

Scene two: a group of children gather excitedly around one of their fellows who is describing graphically something he has experienced. Some, wide-eyed, drink in every word, but others, less trusting, question him closely—in fact they go so far as to say they do not believe him. Our storyteller protests, without success, but then as a final challenge says, 'Cross my heart and hope to die.' There is silence. No more questions—not aloud, anyway—for an oath has been taken, and that is a deliberate and definite commitment to the words spoken.

I well remember a fellow employee of the company for which I worked some years ago who had her own version of truth. In fact, we could never believe a word she told us. She lived in a dream world, but as she tried to convince us that what she was telling us could be believed, she would add the words 'honest to God'. That was the sure signal that we were about to be given a very garbled story, for the fact that she was having to bring God into her account was the giveaway—her word could not be trusted! She is not alone. Many are the protestations I have heard when God's name, or variations on it, have been brought into play. The Lord's name is very often taken in vain, and I have at times reminded the person doing so of the relevant section of the Ten Commandments which say, 'Do not use my name for evil purposes, for I, the Lord your God, will punish anyone who misuses my name' (Exodus 20:7 and Deuteronomy 5:11). Usually I get an embarrassed laugh, or an apologetic, 'Oh, don't take me so seriously. I don't mean anything by it, it's just a figure of speech. I'm sorry.' To which my answer is, 'Well, it's not me you should apologize to, is it?'

Although the two scenes described earlier may seem very alike, they are not. In a court of law the requirement is placed upon people to take the oath; it is to emphasize the solemnity of the evidence. It is a sad fact that many people cannot be relied upon to tell the truth, and do not recognize its importance; so that importance has to be brought home by the weight of law, and by the constraint of the law of perjury. It is recognized that human nature is sinful, deceitful, 'bent'. There are Christians who believe that the words of Jesus, 'Do not use any vow when you make a promise,' are to be obeyed literally, and who refuse to take an oath in court, and they must be respected for their view. In particular the Quakers take this stand. But I believe that there is more to these words of Jesus than the taking of legal oaths.

Think of our young oath-taker in scene two, or of my fellow employee. With them, it was a voluntary act of trying to bolster up their stories by bringing in God, trusting that his name would tip the scales of opinion. I well remember that the wilder my colleague's stories were, the more often would God's name be brought into the conversation. He was 'used' to advance the cause of evil and deceit, and that is surely more serious than perjury in the highest court in our land.

Jesus knew all about legal contortions. He knew the lengths to which men and women would go, the loopholes they would leave for themselves by the way their words were embellished with fancy phrasing, a sprinkling of fine-sounding religious expressions, empty and hollow promises and assurances of as much value as a pile of counterfeit notes. As he looked at the crowd before him, he saw the deceived and the deceivers, the plausible, the perplexed, the cunning and the conned. Jesus spoke simply, directly:

> You have also heard that people were told in the past, 'Do not break your promise, but do what you have vowed to the Lord to do.' But now I tell you: do not use any vow when you make a promise. Do not swear by heaven, because it is God's throne; nor by earth, because it is the resting place for his feet; not by Jerusalem, because it is the city of the great King. Do not even swear by your head, because you cannot make a single hair white or black. Just say 'Yes' or 'No'—anything else you say comes from the Evil One.

If only when we said 'Yes' we meant yes, and when we said 'No' we meant no! But have you ever been asked to do something and have known perfectly well you had no intention of doing it, but you have said something like this: 'I will pray about it and let you know,' or, 'I will think it over and get in touch with you later.' Of course it is right to pray about our actions, to ask for guidance, and expect it. But often we cover up our own selfish reasons by coating our answer with pious-sounding language. We are hypocritical humbugs—we dishonour God, and rightly stand under judgment if our words are not a true reflection of our wills.

All our words, our promises included, are heard by God. We cannot play silly games with him. He sees through our deviousness, our delaying tactics. Whether we call them white lies, it makes no difference; a lie is a lie, not something on a paint colour chart. We are called to be men and women who can be relied on, whose word is their bond; all promises are sacred because they are made in the presence of God. Knowing this should make a difference to every conversation we hold, every letter we write, every telephone call we make.

As we open our eyes to each new day, before we open our

mouths to refuel our bodies with that well-known 'sunshine breakfast', or the latest in health-giving whole grains, we would do well to pray as the psalmist did:

> *May my words and my thoughts be acceptable to you,*
> *O Lord, my refuge and my redeemer (Psalm 19:14).*

Balancing the books

Matthew 5:38—42

A television documentary programme on the work of the war correspondents during World War II brought back childhood memories of 'going to the pictures' during those war years, and seeing the news on the big screen. Two of those newsreels in particular, both seen at the end of the war in Europe, are as vivid in my mind today as they were then, and still produce in me the same feelings as when I first saw them.

The first was the horrendous sight of Belsen concentration camp. As I saw those match-like figures in striped uniforms, the big staring eyes, the piles of bodies, the buildings where such ghastly deeds had been carried out by human beings on other human beings, I felt a revulsion and anger which I had never before experienced in my life. I remember thinking, 'I wish I had never seen this, I shall never forget it'—and I never have. I came out of the cinema and was sick, and I was not the only one. I hated the Germans then with an intensity that nothing before had stirred me to, not even seeing the city of Manchester being bombed, the red sky, and the dull thud of bombs.

The second newsreel that made a lasting impression was of the liberation of France. We saw the troops waving, being given flowers and kisses, the cheering crowds welcoming the Allies—and then a scene of violence, women being dragged along the ground, their heads being shaved, fear in their eyes, and hatred on the faces of those who abused them. I remember the commentator telling us calmly that these were women who had collaborated with the enemy, and now they were being punished by those who had suffered at the hands of the occupying power. What frightened me was the way it seemed to be accepted that people should behave in that way; that it should be classed as justice—they had 'got what was coming to them'. Again I came out of the cinema and was sick, but I never told anyone why, for it would not have done to have expressed sympathy for the enemy, not after all they had done. As a youngster I did not understand what it was all about, but I instinctively felt that there must be a better way for human beings to settle differences than that, for it seemed to reduce them all to the level of animals.

The years pass, human nature does not change. Revenge, they say, is sweet, to be taken, stirred, enjoyed to the full; though in reality it is bitter and poisons the mind and the heart. Northern Ireland stands as a monument to that fact. Tit for tat, blow for blow, death for death, like an awful accounts ledger, with blood-red ticks against corresponding debits and credits, making sure the figures tally at the end; except that there is no end, only 'balance carried forward'. No one has the will-power to draw the lines, and write 'account closed'. But then, what were those words that came ringing out from the Old Testament, often quoted in defence of retaliation: 'An eye for an eye, and a tooth for a tooth'?

'An eye for an eye, and a tooth for a tooth' made sense in its original context. It made for a well-ordered society. It stopped things getting out of hand, by limiting those who would have taken revenge in even more horrific measures. The wandering people of Israel would never have survived their long trek had they not been subject to very stringent rules. Otherwise it would have been survival not only of the fittest and biggest, but of the toughest and roughest, the ones who carried the heaviest punch, or who could outwit their neighbour; it would have been the law of the jungle. The laws of Moses were very specific, covering every aspect of life: sexual behaviour, rules of hygiene, eating habits, farming methods, monetary transactions, business agreements, legal penalties, religious observance, business agreements, legal penalties, religious observance, relationships within the family, in the community, with friends and with foes. These were laws of restraint, not of repression. They were designed for protection.

For those who broke the rules, the law came into play, and

penalties were exacted. What you took away from a person was taken away from you: knock his tooth out, and one of yours would be yanked out; poke his eye out in a fight, then yours would be removed also. No more, no less. There are many parts of the world today where thieves have their hands amputated, where public executions are still carried out—'a life for a life'. We see, too, over and over again, people taking the law into their own hands, meting out their own punishment to those who have offended against them. We may throw up our hands in horror at this rough justice, but how does a victim feel about the one who has inflicted pain and injury? What if you were the victim; if it was your child who had been the subject of an assault; if your mother had been mugged by a young hooligan, your husband run down by a drunken driver? Would you be tempted to strike back if you could get your hands on the offender? I am pretty sure most of us would.

Many of the people who listened to Jesus on the hillside knew at first hand what it was like to be pushed around, taken advantage of, trodden on. After all, they were under an army of occupation. Life was hard; it was every man for himself, and people who were soft went under. The few rights they had they clung to grimly. So what had Jesus to say to them? What comfort would he give them?

> You have heard that it was said, 'An eye for an eye, and a tooth for a tooth.' But now I tell you: do not take revenge on someone who wrongs you. If anyone slaps you on the right cheek, let him slap your left cheek too. And if someone takes you to court to sue you for your shirt, let him have your coat as well. And if one of the occupation troops forces you to carry his pack one kilometre, carry it two kilometres. When someone asks you for something, give it to him; when someone wants to borrow something, lend it to him.

We may not get slapped on the face every day, but most of us are subjected to varying degrees of rudeness, insinuations, snide remarks, offensive language. I find that when that happens I am very tempted to hit back—hard. There's a children's rhyme which says, 'Sticks and stones may break my bones, but words will never hurt me'—but I find that words can hurt far more than sticks or stones or slaps.

I've witnessed some pretty awful scenes between people who claim on the one hand to be brothers and sisters in Christ, yet are downright rude to one another, and indulge in insult-throwing— and sadly, I have to plead guilty myself. Unfortunately it builds up, so that what began as perhaps a slight insult finishes up in a major battle. There is only one way to stop this progression and that is to accept what happens, and not retaliate—to be able to let it bounce off, to 'turn the other cheek', to offer the hand of friend-ship in that situation.

Why? Peter, writing his first letter, says why! 'Christ himself suf-fered for you and left you an example, so that you would follow in his steps. He committed no sin, and no one ever heard a lie come from his lips. When he was insulted, he did not answer back with an insult; when he suffered, he did not threaten, but placed his hopes in God, the righteous Judge' (1 Peter 2:21–23).

Jesus was abused, slapped, insulted and did not retaliate. Yet it was no sign of weakness, but of strength. It takes a big man, a big woman, to be as vulnerable as that. Sadly, we are often so very small, so protective of our rights. Yet until we learn to accept the slaps, we will be of little use as representatives of our Lord.

But what about our rights—we must have some, surely? Of course we do, and most of us make sure we get them! Yet there is nothing more pathetic than seeing people standing on their rights. Every organization has such people; every church has them too! How soon the press picks up the stories of the bickering which goes on when people in the churches, who should know better, get on their 'high horses' about their rights—the rows between vicars and organists; disputes about who sits where, and who does what; those who feel slighted because they were not consulted over a matter, whose position has not been recognized. If some of these situations which sadly make the newspapers were not so tragic, they would be laughable.

We all need to learn to laugh at ourselves, to stop taking our-selves so seriously. I wonder what God thinks as he sees us strut-ting and demanding, building our own flimsy empires which will come crashing down like a pack of cards. We are imprisoned by our own self-images. As we grab and clutch to ourselves what we consider is ours, we shrivel and die; it is only as we can open our hands and our hearts and generously release what we have, freely and unreservedly, that we can begin to grow, to know real freedom.

As we go that second mile, it may give us time to build a relationship, to discover mutual interests, to share burdens and break down barriers. As we lend to others, and give of our substance, we may well find that our poverty of spirit is blessed by the richness that comes from willing obedience.

What is this thing called love?

Matthew 5:43—48

'Love' is the most overworked word in the English language. It can be used to describe the height of sexual ecstasy, the emotion a mother feels for her child, the relationship of a boy with his first motor bike, or the pleasurable sensation of a favourite brand of canned drink.

The best descriptions I know are given by an apostle and a cartoonist! Paul, writing to the Christians in Corinth, put it like this:

> *Love is patient and kind; it is not jealous or conceited or proud; love is not ill-mannered or selfish or irritable; love does not keep a record of wrongs; love is not happy with evil, but is happy with the truth. Love never gives up; and its faith, hope and patience never fail (1 Corinthians 13:4–8).*

Many of us will remember the cartoonist Kim, who described love graphically in the relationship between two small naked figures. They put what Paul says into practice in such mundane ways as remembering what brand of sweets she likes, laughing at his old jokes, helping her with a disliked chore and cooking his favourite meal.

Love is both emotional and practical. Love is the feeling and the doing. Love is declared to be of the heart, the centre of life, the 'gut reaction'.

We love our friends because we feel pleasure in their company; we appreciate their love for us, they are good to us, and we are good to them. They want the very best for us, and go to great lengths so that we may enjoy life, so naturally we do the same for them. We hardly need to be reminded to love our nearest and dearest, those who are like us, who make life pleasant for us, whose companionship we enjoy.

... But there are some people for whom we feel revulsion, dislike and even hatred. It may be something they once said or did, or just the look of them, the cut of their jaw. They may 'have it in' for us, make life difficult or even quite unbearable. Or they go out of their way to humiliate, hurt and anger us. Sometimes it may be even more desperate; we know their aim is to destroy us.

What do we do in such a situation, whether it is the pinpricks that annoy us or the long knives that threaten us? If we want to avoid confrontation, then maybe we feel the best way is isolation: keep out of their way. What do I do as a Christian?

You have heard that it was said, 'Love your friends, hate your enemies.' But now I tell you: love your enemies and pray for those who persecute you, so that you may become the sons of your Father in heaven. For he makes his sun to shine on bad and good people alike, and gives rain to those who do good and to those who do evil. Why should God reward you if you love only the people who love you? Even the tax collectors do that! And if you speak only to your friends, have you done anything out of the ordinary? Even the pagans do that! You must be perfect—just as your Father in heaven is perfect!

Jesus leaves us in no doubt: love them and pray for them! But... but... but... *But* that is what he says. There is no way round it. There is no way of wriggling out of his command—love and pray. But is it possible?

Corrie ten Boom went through indescribable suffering in the concentration camp of Ravensbrück, and she also had to witness the degradation and death of those she loved, including her sister. Her story, *The Hiding Place*, describes those suffering years, and if anyone had cause to hate the brutal prison guards, she had. She describes a meeting after the war with a former guard. He held out his hand to her, and she wrote afterwards:

> I who had preached so often to the people in Bloemendaal the need to forgive, kept my hand at my side. Even as the angry vengeful thoughts boiled through me, I saw the sin of them. Jesus Christ had died for this man; was I going to ask for more? Lord Jesus, I prayed, forgive me, and help me to forgive him. I tried to smile, I struggled to raise my hand. I could not. I felt nothing, not the slightest prick of warmth or charity. And so again I breathed a silent prayer. Jesus, I cannot forgive him. Give me Your forgiveness. As I took his hand the most incredible thing happened. From my shoulder along my arm and through my hand a current seemed to pass from me to him, while into my heart sprang a love for this stranger that almost overwhelmed me. And so I discovered that it is not on our forgiveness any more than on our goodness that the world's healing hinges, but on His. When He tells us to love our enemies, He gives, along with the command, the love itself.

Corrie found out that it is possible not only to forgive but to love. But she had first to make that effort of actually putting out her hand; that was the act of obedience to Jesus Christ's command. She did not feel anything until she obeyed. The trouble is, we want to feel before we act. Until we feel the emotion of love we are not prepared to do anything loving, because we are not super-human, we are just ordinary men and women who give as good, or as bad, as we get. Why should we love other people? John gives us the answer in his first letter when he says, 'This is what love is: it is not that we have loved God, but that he loved us and sent his Son to be the means by which our sins are forgiven. Dear friends, if this is how God loved us, then we should love one another' (1 John 4:10–11).

The love has been supplied; we have to connect it up. Then the current of love has its effect, not only on the one who is being loved, but on the other, that ordinary human being, you or me, who in obedience—loves.

Coretta King, the widow of the late Martin Luther King, the American civil rights leader, suffered decades of abuse, threats and violence. Her late husband's character is still attacked, as many seek to discredit him. Even death did not bring an end to the campaign of hate. And yet she could say in an interview: 'Of course you get feelings of anger, because you are only human. It's not easy to love people who hate you and misuse you. You have to work at it, but time and again I have seen how it has transformed those who have opposed us.'

Corrie ten Boom and Coretta King—just two who could bear witness to the power of love and forgiveness over hatred and bitterness. Faced with such examples, doesn't it make our puny efforts look feeble? Shouldn't it make us resolve to put out our hand in forgiveness, to respond lovingly in the face of unfairness?

When we look at the cross and see how Jesus reacted to those who put him there—to the men who hammered in the nails, who shouted abuse as he agonized, laughed as he bled, swore at him as he prayed—can we refuse to obey his command to love our enemies?

Jesus says we are to 'be perfect, just as your Father in heaven is perfect'. Now that is impossible—isn't it? Frail, ordinary, sinful human beings like us, told to be perfect—we can't do it. No, not just as frail, ordinary, sinful human beings; but as those who have received the love of Jesus, who are filled with his Spirit, it is gloriously possible.

When I was a youngster I joined an organization run by a magazine, called The Golden Star Brigade. The motto was 'Look up, and aim high'. I don't know what happened to that particular organization, but 'Look up and aim high' is a good motto for all of us, whatever our age. We look at Jesus, and make our aim to be like him. Of course we are not going to make it this side of heaven, but as my vicar is always telling me, 'We have to aim at the moon even if we only hit the haystack.' And there is another saying: 'Practice makes perfect.' So let's practise our loving—and there is one thing for sure, we are not going to run out of raw material to practise on, are we? And it might help us if we prayed as Augustine did:

Give what thou commandest,
And command what thou wilt.

Charity — sweet charity

Matthew 6:1—4

There are some requirements which are common to every religion, and giving to the poor and needy has always ranked high in the obligation stakes. The expectation is that, having obeyed the letter of the religious law, the giver will be rewarded by God in due time. It is also assumed that God pays a generous interest rate, so it pays to pay up. The book of Proverbs has this to say on the subject: 'When you give to the poor, it is like lending to the Lord, and the Lord will pay you back' (Proverbs 19:17). If you assume that, you can do quite nicely out of it in this life. 'Give to the poor and you will never be in need,' says Proverbs 28:27, which makes giving a sensible proposition, and it follows up with a warning: 'If you close your eyes to the poor, many people will curse you.' And no one wants that to happen—it could be nasty!

So there was no argument about the good sense of being charitable, it was one of those religious duties that was accepted quite happily. After all, as God was well aware of all that went on, he would be entering up the merit points in his big ledger for a later paying-out day!

Doing good can be so very dull, though, even if you know it is right and proper and trust that God has taken note of your kindness. So it is so much more enjoyable if there are people around to witness your good deeds. Make sure that you speak loudly as you give to the beggar, and ensure that the light catches the coin as you pass it over with a flourish. Tell your friends how well you have observed the law of charity today, then they will recognize your worth, slap you on the back, praise your generosity, tell their friends about you, and your standing in the community will rise. All this is very satisfactory; it will make you feel good, warm, happy, important, valued. In fact it is a most rewarding feeling. Rather like being the hero in the play, taking the leading role in the stage performance, playing to the audience, earning their approval, delighting in the applause, taking the curtain calls.

As Jesus looked at the crowd before him, those who would be well aware of their religious duties, he had words of warning for them. Words that would pull them up sharp as he probed into the motives which lay behind their religious observances. Words that are equally addressed to you and me as we put our hands into our pockets, open our purses, or reach for our pen and cheque book.

Make certain you do not perform your religious duties in public so that people will see what you do. If you do these things publicly, you will not have any reward from your Father in heaven.

So when you give something to a needy person, do not make a big show of it, as the hypocrites do in the houses of worship and on the streets. They do it so that people will praise them. I assure you, they have already been paid in full. But when you help a needy person, do it in such a way that even your closest friend will not know about it. Then it will be a private matter. And your Father, who sees what you do in private, will reward you.

I can imagine that, as Jesus said this, there were a few puzzled looks and furrowed brows, and a bit of murmuring going on in the back rows. Maybe a bright spark in the front chipped in, 'But *you* just said we were to shine like lights, so other people would see the good things we do and praise our Father in heaven. How can we shine secretly?'—a question that has been raised many times in the last two thousand years, but it is a very red herring! What Jesus is warning about is making a show of our giving, a song and dance about our charity. He is talking about motives.

What is your motive for giving? I suppose all our motives are mixed, but what is our prime motive? Anne Daltrop in her book *Charities* asks that question, and comes up with a very comprehensive answer:

The motives for giving to charity in our day are as varied as they have always been. Apart from generosity, people may give to create good will, out of pity, to gain power over others, to avoid embarrassment or suspicion of meanness. Sometimes good causes are supported for political reasons, or to preserve certain values and attitudes in which the donor himself believes, for social reasons or for fame.

Most of us give from a mixture of these motives. For some givers, the result is what they hoped for: a medal, a plaque on the wall, a photograph in the local paper, a round of applause—so what? They deserved their reward, and got it. But most people are genuinely surprised when they are praised or rewarded; their motives were high, they did not expect a reward. Knowing that they have done the right thing according to their conscience is enough recompense. We should not despise rewards if they come, but neither should we allow them to cloud our vision by setting out to gain in personal status through good works and charitable behaviour.

King David in the Bible was the outstanding God-fearing king, and he also made many mistakes. His motives were mixed in his religious life, political leadership and personal dealings; but he loved God, and recognized that everything he had came as a gift from God. At the end of his reign he reminded his people and himself of this, giving God the glory.

You are great and powerful, glorious, splendid, and majestic.
Everything in heaven and earth is yours, and you are king,
supreme ruler over all. All riches and wealth come from you; you
rule everything by your strength and power; and you are able to
make anyone great and strong. Now, our God, we give you
thanks, and we praise your glorious name.

Yet my people and I cannot really give you anything, because
everything is a gift from you, and we have only given back what
is yours already (1 Chronicles 29:11–14).

King David had got it right! He gave God the glory, and so giving was a privilege, an act of worship.

Is your giving an act of worship? If we had the words of King David written on our hearts, the church would have no financial problems, and the charities would not have to employ so many fundraisers to ensure that the hungry are fed, the needy cared for. We would not see people sleeping rough in our cities, or without the basic requirements to live a decent life. If we call ourselves followers of Jesus Christ, then we must obey what he says, and our lives must reflect him. That will affect what we put in the offertory plate on Sunday, or the collecting tin on Saturday's flag day; what we give for the work of the church overseas, and our contribution to help alleviate the vast needs in the world. It will affect the way we treat our neighbours, how we use our time, even our tone of voice as we reply to someone asking for our help. It will also open our eyes to see need, and open our heart to respond. Everything we have is a gift from God. That includes our cash and our car, our telephone and our time.

I have a friend who is a great help to me in many different ways. Whatever I have needed he has given me gladly, be it encouragement when I have felt low, a helping hand with my car, a listening ear to my moans—and he even warms my cassock on the radiator in the vestry on cold Sunday mornings! His response to my thanks is, 'It's a pleasure.' He spends his life giving. Some people appreciate him, others do not; some even think him a fool for being 'soft', and mostly he is just taken for granted. The fact that the giving of himself is costly for him in so many ways is probably not realized by many people, yet he can still say, and mean, 'It's a pleasure,' because for him it is a pleasure to give. If you asked him why, I have no doubt of the answer. It would be because of the joy of knowing Jesus Christ. He has a grateful, giving heart, which sees service as a pleasure, obedience as a privilege.

Call it religious duty, charity or almsgiving, it is all these things, but more. What it really amounts to is love. As we learn to love through being loved, then we will neither keep account of our giving, nor ask that others might take account of it. Giving will be a 'labour of love'.

Teach us, good Lord, to serve thee as thou deservest;
to give, and not to count the cost,
to fight, and not to heed the wounds,
to toil, and not to seek for rest,
to labour, and not to ask for any reward
save that of knowing that we do thy will.

(Ignatius Loyola, 1491–1556)

Look at me — I'm praying!

Matthew 6:5—8

There are surveys carried out on every topic under the sun. You have probably been stopped in the street by an anxious-looking young lady with a clipboard who says, 'Would you mind answering a few questions? We are carrying out a survey on...' or confronted by a questionnaire which promises both confidentiality and a small reward for putting ticks into appropriate boxes. I suspect that many answers are given very much tongue-in-cheek, and that the validity of the answers depends on the weather and the state of mind the interviewee happens to be in at that precise moment.

Still, bearing this in mind, I am always interested to read the results of surveys, and when one was conducted on religious beliefs I took note of some of the findings. It was interesting to discover that most people claim to pray at some time, even those who find it difficult to believe in God. It seems to be a shout of, 'If anyone is out there, help!' When the going gets hard, and no one else seems able to help, then it is hoped there is a God, and a God who will listen.

Jesus assumed that the people who sat listening to him did pray, for he said, '*When* you pray...' Of course, all Jews prayed. It was part of their cultural and religious inheritance, and a requirement laid upon them. There were prayers for all times and all occasions, at set times and in set ways. The hours of 9 a.m., 12 noon and 3 p.m. were amongst those when the devout Jew must stop and pray, and even in those days, although they did not have our 'rush hours', it would be likely that many people would be milling around and could see who were the pray-ers. There would be quite a temptation to gain 'maximum coverage' by being sure to be in a prominent place at these times, and going on at length in case of being missed; and so that the hard of hearing would not miss out on what was happening, the gestures would be elaborate. It would be so easy to put on an act, and play to the gallery, in order to give an impression of holiness and piety.

Jesus knew all about such people. He saw them and saw through them. They got what they wanted most—acclaim. Their motive was to get praise, and they received it, but from human beings, not from God.

People at prayer may all look the same, go through the same motions and say the same words; but what matters is who they are addressing. Some prayers could be merely a personal public address system, a show of prayer for those around. Maybe the words are beautiful; there is eloquence, drama and movement, and the timing is perfect; but unless the prayers are in response to the greatness of God, coming before him in praise, penitence and adoration, they are not true prayer.

The Jews had their sacred times of prayer; there would be those who used those times to the glory of God, others to self-glory. We may not down tools at nine, twelve and three o'clock—although there are tea-breaks some would hold sacred! But what about 11 a.m. and 6.30 p.m. on Sundays? As we come into church, where are our thoughts directed? Towards God, or towards ourselves, or to what others are thinking of us? Are we always so far removed from the hypocrites, the 'play actors' Jesus refers to? Whether we bow or genuflect, kneel, sit, or stand with our arms in the air, are we really praying or playing? What about all those elaborate and very beautiful forms of worship we join in? Could they ever be described by Jesus as 'meaningless words' because of the way we have used them? What about the evangelical prayer meeting, when the élite, the 'spiritually mature', gather—when we think we have got prayer all buttoned up and ours is *the* way to pray? How often in such a meeting do we go on a tour of the world, taking in also our neighbours' sins and shortcomings, and reminding God of our own achievements? Could it be that Jesus was referring to people like you and me when he spoke about those who thought God would hear them because of their long prayers? Jesus had something to say to that kind of person when he told the story of the two men who went up to the temple to pray—the one who told God what a good man he was, the other who asked for forgiveness. It's worth reading again that story in Luke 18:9–14. What a lot to ponder on in those few verses!

Why did Jesus speak so plainly about the misuse of prayer? Surely, because he wants us to discover the real joy of prayer, to know that close relationship with God as Father, and not to settle for a very second best of trying to make an impression on people. Jesus prayed publicly as well as privately, and those who saw him at prayer realized that his praying was different from anyone else's. They saw the beauty of a relationship, and their response was to ask him to teach them to pray. That was the effect Jesus at prayer had. What effect does our praying have on others who see and hear us? Has anyone ever asked you, 'Please teach me to pray, I see what a difference it makes to you'? Seeing us at prayer can turn people on to God, or off him—which does it do?

When Jesus spoke so directly to the Samaritan woman at the well, she tried to divert him by entering into a theological discussion about the place to worship. His reply came swiftly and to the point: 'God is Spirit, and only by the power of his Spirit can people worship him as he really is' (John 4:24).

It is not the place we are seen in, the words we use or the posture we adopt that is the essential of prayer, but in our relationship with God the Father through Jesus Christ in the power of the Holy Spirit.

A member of our church who is a busy wife and mother, up to her eyes in all sorts of good work both in the church and the town, once said to me wistfully, 'I'd like to be a nun.' When I laughed and told her I didn't really think she would be accepted, and asked why this sudden urge to leave home for a convent, she said, 'I just want the peace and quiet to be with God. We rush around so much, we never give God a chance to speak to us.' She is right. We dash from this to that, from here to there, in and out. We would find our lives so different if only we would do what Jesus tells us to do: 'Go to your room, close the door and pray to your Father...' We don't have to go into a convent, leave our homes and families or drop our activities to do this; but we must make very sure that we do spend time alone with God.

We need to shut the door on the world and open up to God. I find personally that being alone in a church is a marvellous way of taking sanctuary from all that would divert me away from prayer. Or sometimes I drive out into the country and walk up a hill, peacefully and alone. I find that prayer and praise come easily when I am riding my bicycle down a country lane. I cannot help but pray when I am surrounded by all the evidence of God's grace in the beauty of the natural world, breathing in his love.

And the reward of prayer? For me it is the assurance of his attention, his loving concern, being in his presence—a rich reward indeed, not to be exchanged for anything on earth, for it is beyond price.

Of course, worshipping together formally or informally, in a mighty cathedral or quiet country church, in a prayer meeting, in a house or with a couple of friends over a coffee break, are ways of prayer we must value and use, because as Christians we are a family, and we come together as a family to meet with our Father. But this is not to say to others, 'See how good we are, how well we pray', but to express our joy and delight in God's presence, to share together in bringing people and situations to him and to give him all the glory.

Prayer is such a tremendous gift that we must use it with love and reverence. So let's not play at it, but enter into it, coming to meet with our Father in 'wonder, love and praise'.

The words Jesus speaks to those who pray are words of warning and also of promise.

Let us take heed of both!

When you pray, do not be like the hypocrites! They love to stand up and pray in the houses of worship and on the street corners, so that everyone will see them. I assure you, they have already been paid in full. But when you pray, go to your room, close the door, and pray to your Father, who is unseen. And your Father, who sees what you do in private, will reward you.

When you pray, do not use a lot of meaningless words, as the pagans do, who think that God will hear them because their prayers are long. Do not be like them. Your father already knows what you need before you ask him.

The family way

Matthew 6:9—15

My family are always complaining about the fact that books are taking over the house. They are everywhere. We have bookcases in almost every room, mainly to contain my collection, for I collect books like some people collect stamps or postcards. Whenever I go into a bookshop I gravitate to the section marked 'prayer'. This is not because I am an expert in prayer—sadly, quite the opposite. I find it hard to pray with so much crowding in upon my mind, demanding my attention. I am very easily distracted from what I know I should do, and so I buy yet another book on prayer, hoping it will provide me with the formula I need. I read the lives of great pray-ers and feel ashamed of my paltry offering of time. I marvel at the eloquence of written prayers, and I seize upon the latest offerings of advice on the life of prayer. I long to fill my life with prayer, but so often settle for filling the shelves of my bookcases with books on the subject, which is a very poor alternative to the real thing, actually praying.

The first disciples of Jesus had no such facilities as I have, no fingertip selection of do-it-yourself prayer guides. But they had the Master of prayer with them. They could ask, 'Teach us to pray'—and they did; and his response to their request was not a reading list or a theory to examine but a model to follow.

This, then is how you should pray:
'Our Father in heaven:

May your holy name be honoured:
may your Kingdom come;
may your will be done on earth as it is in heaven.
Give us today the food we need.
Forgive us the wrongs we have done,
as we forgive the wrongs that others have done to us.
Do not bring us to hard testing,
but keep us safe from the Evil One.

Plain, simple, short. The prayer a child can say, the prayer that is used in almost every public act of worship, that is said at the baptism of a child, at a marriage service and at funerals. It is said by countless millions privately, the family prayer in many homes, the prayer that binds together Christians of every denomination, often the last prayer said by a dying man or woman.

It is the family prayer which binds together all those who through Jesus have come to realize that God is their Father, and who knows that others are their brothers and sisters, children of the same Father. It is an intensely personal prayer, and it is the prayer of fellowship in united prayer and worship. It is the prayer that dissolves barriers and builds bridges. It is a gift, the gift of Jesus to those who are serious about prayer.

If my bookcases with all those helpful, beautiful, theological, philosophical views on prayer were to go up in flames tomorrow, if I was cast away on a desert island without even the guaranteed two books for every castaway on *Desert Island Discs*—the Bible and the complete works of Shakespeare—I would still have all I needed, the Lord's Prayer learned by heart.

Could it be that one day memory, for a variety of reasons, might fail; would it matter if I got the prayer muddled, if in my confusion I was not even able to say it? I have been with people in their last moments, visited those whose mind and memory have gone, and yet, as I have taken their hand and said the Lord's prayer, I have seen their lips move, mouthing the words, though often voicelessly. Learned by heart, it has become part of the heart, which goes on beyond the mind, and God knows the heart better than the one in whose frail body it beats.

When we visit the elderly, or the frail in body or mind, we so often think we can do nothing for them. We offer the bunch of flowers, plump up their cushions and talk about the weather, and come away feeling useless. My experience is that the greatest gift we can give them is to take their hand and say the Lord's prayer. It is an act of love and obedience to our Lord's command, 'When you pray, say...'

Richard Wurmbrand, a Romanian Christian pastor, was imprisoned and tortured for his faith. Everything was done to break his spirit. Starved, beaten, drugged, he got to the point when he forgot almost everything, even how to speak. He could not remember words of scripture. He tried to say the Lord's prayer and couldn't remember it; he could only get as far as 'Our Father, which art in heaven, hallowed be thy name...' and he says this in his chapter in *My Path of Prayer*.

> *I was very sad. The Son of God came from heaven to earth to teach us this prayer, so it must be important to know it. What would I do now that I had forgotten his words? Very soon a comforting thought came. I had forgotten the prayer, but I knew which prayer I had forgotten: one beginning with the assertion that he who rules heaven is my Father. I need not worry. Folding my hands I said, 'Our Father which art in heaven, I have forgotten the prayer, but surely by this time you know it by heart. You have heard it so many times. Consider that I have said it. I love you, Amen.'*

Pastor Richard Wurmbrand was to remain in that state for a long time, but God did not desert him. His Father held on to him, and he was able to say this: 'One day I discovered that I could say again the "Our Father". It was like awaking out of a swoon. Every word was new to me, and full of depth.'

Perhaps none of us will ever have to suffer like Richard Wurmbrand, but there are times when we feel we cannot pray, not even the Lord's prayer—maybe though grief, depression, anger, or confusion, at times when we are broken hearted, when we shout, 'Why has this happened?' If then we can only manage to say, 'Our Father', then we put ourselves into our Father's hands. 'The atom releases energy only when it is split. The broken heart and its prayer *in extremis* has a tremendous force'—again Richard Wurmbrand, speaking from the experience of a heart broken, and a heart mended by 'Our Father'.

Often when we pray, we come to our Father like the whining children sometimes seen—and heard—in the supermarket: 'I want!' 'Why can't I?' Yell, kick, scream. 'I want my own way, and I want it right *now*!' But if we follow the model Jesus gave us, then we should be coming to give God the glory, praising him for who he is; for he is not just a Father, or our Father, but our Father who is in heaven, who is King, who rules over heaven and earth. We come as his children *and* as his subjects. We come asking that we might do what he wants us to do, for it is his kingdom that matters, not our selfish demands. 'You have to get your priorities right'—how many times have you heard that said, or said it yourself? I know I have! And what we are praying in the Lord's prayer is that we should make God's priorities our priorities, for then we shall know we are going in the right direction.

After that we can bring our needs: the needs we have for sustaining our life, our 'daily bread'. We ask for strength which comes through knowing we are in a right relationship with him and with others, asking for forgiveness for our sins, and being reminded that we are to forgive others freely and unreservedly as we wish to be forgiven ourselves. We come asking for our Father's protection, for deliverance out of the evil that would drag us down. We bring ourselves, our lives, before him. We pray for our needs today, for forgiveness for the past and for strength for tomorrow—and we can ask in real confidence because he is our Father.

'Our' Father—so when we pray that prayer, we pray with all the family of God; it is not 'my' and 'mine'. And so we find ourselves charged with answering that prayer for help, for bread, for forgiveness, for protection. The weak members of the family are also the responsibility of the stronger brothers and sisters as well as of our Father. We can never look at a situation or person, however far away or near to us, and say, 'They are nothing to do with me', because if we pray the Lord's prayer we are acknowledging that they have everything to do with us—they are part of the family. It is said that 'we choose our friends, but God gives us our relations'. Quite true—we have no choice about our relations; they are tied to us and we to them by blood. We may deny this, forget it, resent it, but that doesn't alter the fact that they are 'family'. We are the family of God 'by blood'—the blood of Jesus who taught us when we pray to say, 'Our Father...'

Jesus adds a very solemn warning after giving the model for our prayers. He says this:

> *If you forgive others the wrongs they have done to you, your*
> *Father in heaven will also forgive you. But if you do not forgive*
> *others, then your Father will not forgive the wrongs*
> *you have done.*

There is a condition placed on being forgiven, and that is that we must forgive others. When we ask for forgiveness we open our hands to receive it, we come 'open-handed'; but if our hand is raised in anger against someone else, or slamming the door in his face, or covering our ears so we will not hear him, or our eyes so we will not see him, then how can God give us anything? We shut out God's forgiveness by our own hand, we deny ourselves the thing we need most. And so we will grow hard and bitter, turned in on ourselves, until we no longer care for anything or anyone... and whose fault will that be? Our own. And that is unforgivable— isn't it?

The warning came to the people sitting on the hillside. It comes to us sitting by the fire, or on the train or plane, or wherever we are at this moment. Thank God we still have time to forgive, and so to know the joy of forgiveness ourselves. And that time is right now.

Keep it secret

Matthew 6:16—18

We have all met the diet bores. They talk endlessly of the latest perfect diet they have discovered—the banana diet, the potato diet, the high-fibre diet. They count every calorie, they flourish their calculators, and inform us with delight that they have kept to one thousand calories today, they have resisted temptation, they are strong and fit.

Their obsession is understandable, for we are constantly being pulled in two directions through the powerful medium of advertising. There are advertisements for convenience foods, exciting drinks, delicious treats, 'naughty but nice' cream cakes. Our high streets boast every variety of fast food takeaways—even before you have entered the supermarkets or have caught a whiff of hot, fresh bread coming from the Home Bakers. Food and drink is packaged so attractively, it is irresistible. Can any of us say we buy only what we need? We all fall for the sales patter, the tempting package. We all succumb to impulse buying, and therefore impulse consuming. 'Naughty but nice' implies we will be naughty, because it is nice!

At the same time we are also being urged to 'fight the flab', to get rid of the inches so we can be sexually attractive, or fit into the fashionable gear; to get into the swing of exercises and athletic pursuits. We are told that all this will lengthen our life, extend our social activities, and give us an entirely new wardrobe. So we purchase this or that diet formula or slimming aid, and change our eating and drinking habits for a low-calorie-value life—'Look better, feel better'.

Many of us swing from one extreme to another. Having succumbed to the temptations, we then try to redress the balance by dieting. 'You win a few and you lose a few' is my personal experience! Usually we make a great song and dance about what we are giving up or cutting out, and keep very quiet indeed about what we are taking in, and what we have put on!

When Jesus talked about fasting, he did not mean dieting. The trouble is, we equate the two; and although if we fast we will probably do ourselves a lot of good physically, that was not what Jesus was talking about. The people listening to him knew what he meant when he talked about fasting because it was part of their religious way of life. It was accepted, if you were a Jew, that you fasted on particular days and within certain times. There was no 'if you fast', but 'when you fast', and he gave them this warning:

> *And when you fast, do not put on a sad face as the hypocrites do. They neglect their appearance so that everyone will see that they are fasting. I assure you, they have already been paid in full. When you go without food, wash your face and comb your hair, so that others cannot know that you are fasting—only your Father, who is unseen, will know. And your Father, who sees what you do in private, will reward you.*

Jesus had very stern words of warning for those who performed their religious duties in public. As with giving and praying, fasting was also something to be done as an offering to God and not as a proud public gesture—'Look at me, how good I am!—inviting acclaim and applause. No doubt when we do such things publicly we will be admired, thought spiritual, and our names will rise to the top of the list for positions of authority and leadership within the community and church. After all, anyone can see how generous, prayerful and disciplined we are; what a good thing there are still people like us! Of course, our lives will reflect our faith, and James reminds us in his letter that we must prove our faith by our actions; but it is our motive that matters, not the outward appearance. We are reminded of that many times in scripture, and, as God said to Samuel when he sent him to anoint a son of Jesse as king of Israel and Samuel had the choice of many fine, handsome young men, 'I do not judge as man judges. Man looks at the outward appearance, but I look at the heart' (1 Samuel 16:7). David was the youngest, least important son, but God saw the heart of the man David. God's orders of priority are often so very different from ours!

So we are well and truly warned about the ways we give and pray and fast. But remember, Jesus said, '*When* you...' Fasting is biblical. It is important, not least because Jesus himself practised it. And perhaps in our 'If you want it, have it' society, when we have become accustomed to having our wants instantly satisfied, it would be advisable for us to rediscover the value of fasting, and practise it.

Richard Foster, in his book *Celebration of Discipline*, has some very helpful advice. He says this: 'To use good things to our own ends is always the sign of false religion. How easy it is to take something like fasting and try to use it to get God to do what we want... Fasting must for ever centre on God. It must be God-initiated and God-ordained.' He then goes on to say, 'More than any other single discipline, fasting reveals the things that control us. This is a wonderful benefit to the true disciple who longs to be transformed into the image of Jesus Christ... Fasting helps us keep our balance in life.'

Why we fast is a matter between us and God. It may be so that we can give him our total attention with all our being. It may be so that we can draw closer to him in prayer and worship. It may be as an act of penitence or thanksgiving. It may be many things, but it is a personal matter between us and him, always for his glory, and never for ours. He knows our hearts, and will meet with us as we seek to show our love. That, surely, is our reward.

Safer than
the Bank of England

Matthew 6:19—21

After our wedding I carefully and lovingly put away my wedding dress, folded neatly in tissue paper to keep it from creasing. The box was sealed, and like many 'treasures' it was put into the loft of our brand new home. The years went by. The box, intact, was moved from one loft to another. One day our daughter was going to a fancy dress party. 'You can go as a bride,' I said. 'I have the very thing, but you must be careful with it.' The box was brought down from the loft, and the tape removed—only to reveal a heap of something akin to confetti. The moths and the mice had had a field day, or many field days. My treasure was only fit for the dustbin. At least I still had the photographs!

We are all by nature acquisitive; it is part of our search for security. We acquire our treasures, our collections, precious objects which we hope are going to appreciate and therefore provide us with the security we need for a 'rainy day'.

The trouble is, things have a habit of dropping to pieces, rather like my wedding dress. That prized vintage vehicle or model train set gets eroded by rust; and thieves seem to have an uncanny way of knowing just where the valuables are in the house and, however good the locks, seem to be able to get in and steal. Open your local paper today and I guarantee that there will be a number of burglaries reported. It's an everyday occurrence.

There is always the bank, of course, and those precious beautiful heirlooms can be stored away for you... at a fee. But then money devalues, and if you have to keep your beautiful objects locked away for safe keeping, they don't give you much pleasure, do they?

Those attentive listeners to Jesus had no safe deposit boxes or bank accounts, but they, like us, wanted to have security. The trouble was, their beautiful cloth wore out in time and was prone to attack by a variety of insects and creatures—no mothballs in their day! Metals rusted away, and they couldn't always remember where they had buried their treasures—even today some of those buried treasures are still being discovered. It was easy to break into their homes—no burglar alarms or sophisticated locks—and as for carrying around their wealth with them, there was no police force to protect the traveller, bands of robbers roamed the countryside, and nothing was safe.

Yet in spite of the hazards they clung to their possessions, for their varied treasures represented their worth in the world.

Perhaps some of Jesus' listeners carried their material security with them, wearing belts with the coins and valuables hidden under their clothes. They would be careful who they were sitting or standing next to, for in a crowd you never know who might be rubbing up against you; crowds are ideal places for thieves to operate in. So Jesus began to speak about security, a subject dear to all.

Do not store up riches for yourselves here on earth, where moths and rust destroy, and robbers break in and steal. Instead, store up riches for yourselves in heaven, where moths and rust cannot destroy, and robbers cannot break in and steal. For your heart will always be where your riches are.

He offers the perfect protection plan, one hundred per cent proof; no more worry, no danger of disintegration, erosion or theft... just one problem—it's a different sort of currency he is talking about, it's the treasure of heaven.

Where are your riches? I don't suppose you are so foolish as to leave precious material in the loft; though any material can now be treated against moths, it's all so scientific these days. Any DIY shop will offer a variety of rust-proofing, and there is such a thing as insurance. Today our treasures can be safe and secure, with a lifetime's guarantee.

Ah, there's the rub! Sadly, no one can offer us more than a lifetime's guarantee!

I have the sort of memory that remembers rather useless information and silly verses. One such verse goes like this:

> *Use your money while you are living,*
> *Do not hoard it to be proud,*
> *For you cannot take it with you,*
> *There's no pocket in a shroud.*

Not so silly, though, is it? It is absolutely true. We cannot take it with us, we have to leave it all behind. Read the wills of the rich and famous, the not-so-rich and the unknown. Whatever the sum, however much, however little, the words are 'He left...' One day ours will be recorded in the same manner. The problem is, we act as though we do take it with us. Many people have tried, of course. Ancient tombs reveal treasure beyond belief—gold and silver, jewellery, armour, furnishings, even cooking-pots! But they remain for the bounty hunters, or as museum exhibits; their owners have gone, unable to take with them from the grave all they held dear.

Jesus said, 'Store up riches for yourself in heaven.' Now that sounds fine, but what sort of exchange rate is there? What is heavenly currency? What sort of travellers' cheques are available for purchase?

The treasure of heaven is the approval of God, the 'Well done, you good and faithful servant!' Our service for him is done not for gaining merit points, but out of love and obedience. He is our treasure, our priceless treasure, beyond any price we can pay, yet offered to us freely; but in exchange we must give him our heart.

Dietrich Bonhoeffer wrote, 'The heart in the biblical sense is not the inward life, but the whole man in relation to God.' That is, our body, our mind and our spirit; the way we use our life, in whose employ we are, and why. Where is the focus of our activity? Our love? Our aspirations? Our hope?

A young man came to Jesus wanting to know the secret of treasure in heaven, and Jesus told him it was in putting him first, and giving up everything else. Sadly, the young man could not do that, for we are told, 'He went away sad, because he was very rich' (Matthew 19:22). He was more concerned with the currency of earth than the treasure of heaven. He, like us, would have been happy to have had some of each; but it's one or the other, Jesus says, and he leaves the choice entirely to us.

I can only echo the words of John Newton, that great Christian hymn writer and minister who was converted to Jesus Christ while a slave trader in the eighteenth century:

> *Saviour, if of Zion's city*
> *I through grace a member am,*
> *Let the world deride or pity,*
> *I will glory in Thy name;*
> *Fading is the world's best pleasure,*
> *All its boasted pomp and show;*
> *Solid joys and lasting treasure,*
> *None but Zion's children know.*

Do you see?

Matthew 6:22—23

Jesus did not need to spell out for his listeners the tragedy of blindness; the evidence was all around them daily. The blind beggar pleading for help, totally reliant on the goodwill of others, was an object of both pity and scorn. To be blind was to be defenceless, prey to kicks and cuffs or even worse, without any hope of the situation improving. Today it is very different, when the blind are enabled to lead a much more independent life, with special schools, courses, medical attention, encouragement, allowances. Blind people have overcome many obstacles, taking part in sport, earning a living, enjoying hobbies; but it is still a dark and unfriendly world.

Imagine what it must be like not to be able to see the faces of family and friends, to look into a shop window, to watch a film or play, to delight in the colours of the changing seasons, to have the freedom to run for a bus, or to play cricket or football, bringing together the co-ordination of eyes, hands and feet. Some have never known sight, and so cannot even imagine colour and shades. Others, who have lost their sight, or have deficient sight, strain to recapture what was once theirs, living in a blurred, twilight world, which demands almost superhuman effort to cope with what most people take for granted.

How precious are the eyes! What a joy to see the world around us, to take in its delights, to avoid its dangers. Our eyes are the windows on to life. Perhaps we take them too much for granted when we open them each morning to a new day, to light and life!

How marvellous it must have been to have sat in the crowd on the hillside and to have seen Jesus, to have watched his facial expressions, the movements of his body; to have taken in that whole scene, a scene to be recaptured in the mind's eye many times afterwards, recalling his presence; to have been able to say, 'I saw him... I saw him with my own eyes!'

And Jesus began to talk about the value of their eyes:

The eyes are like a lamp for the body. If your eyes are sound, your whole body will be full of light; but if your eyes are no good, your body will be in darkness. So if the light in you is darkness, how terribly dark it will be!

As they looked at him, some would begin to realize that he was not just talking about physical blindness, and the world of darkness that blind people inhabit, but about a far greater darkness— a terrible darkness that afflicts the spirit, that distorts and disfigures the soul, that rejects the light, that blocks out truth. Could it be that *they* were in darkness—that they were the blind he was talking about?

And could it be that we suffer from the same problem? Faulty vision, impaired sight? Do we keep our eyes tightly closed for fear of what we might see? Have we become blind to the reality of God's truth and love?

The account of Jesus healing the man born blind is one of the best-known stories in the New Testament. It has all the ingredients for a drama production, and every Sunday school teacher, Bible class leader and preacher must have used it many, many times. I have lost count of how many times I have preached on the ninth chapter of John's Gospel, and the account just read through without comment has a riveting effect.

It is a story full of people, very different sorts of people, with very different viewpoints on what happened. There are the blind man, his parents and the neighbours. There are the curious onlookers, those who want to know what is going on, and to put in their opinion on the matter. Then there are the religious leaders, the Pharisees. And there is the central figure of Jesus, the healer.

We read of the healing of the blind man, of his gradual awareness of who has healed him, culminating in his personal statement of faith, 'I believe, Lord!' There is the drawing back by his parents, whose joy at having a son who could now see was marred by fear of the authorities; and so they avoided responsibility, washed their hands of him, saying, 'Ask him; he is old enough, and can answer for himself!'—in other words, 'You are on your own, son!' There is the hard, condemning attitude of the Pharisees, who could see no further than the fact that Jesus had broken one of their rules by actually daring to heal a man on the Sabbath—that, to them, was working, and working on the Sabbath was sin!

The central figure is Jesus. He, after all, is the one who has caused the rumpus. What does he think about the reactions? What does he do? You can refresh your memory by reading the account for yourself!

I can never read this story without a degree of personal unease, asking myself, 'Where would I have stood if I had been there?' No doubt I would have been in the front row of onlookers, for I enjoy excitement! I would have wanted to hear all the arguing, add my own bit, and at the end of the day come to a conclusion not just about the man who had been blind, but about the one who had healed him of his blindness. But who would I have sided with? Might it not have been with the Pharisees, the educated leaders, the acknowledged experts in religion? After all, what use were rules and regulations if they were not kept? It could open up all sorts of problems if people did what they liked, and let one healing occur on the Sabbath and before you knew where you were, there would be dozens. No, I fear that with my 'establishment' streak I might well have lent a hand in expelling that fellow who seemed to have got too big for his boots just because he could see.

It's a frightening thought, isn't it? We may be the modern-day version of those Pharisees; we could be as blind as them to what Jesus is doing and saying today. What about when we hear of miracles happening today—do we believe the reports? What of our attitude to those who proclaim the good news in what seems very strange language and garb—do we praise the Lord, or issue disclaimers? It is so easy to quote chapter and verse to back up our own ideas and opinions—to throw out anything we cannot fathom by our own deduction, to close ranks against anyone who does not fit in with us. So easy to be blinded by our own conceit, our vision impaired by pride and envy.

Jesus had this to say to such people: 'If you were blind, then you would not be guilty; but since you claim that you can see, this means that you are still guilty' (John 9:41).

Today we are bombarded by the pronouncements of people in positions of leadership, of scholars who have closely studied the gospel accounts, who tell us that some of the things we have believed all our lives are untrue, or at best poetic licence. These people may hold high positions in the church, have letters after their names, and move in elevated circles—so who do we believe? We may have rejoiced in our 'simple faith', but does it really mean that we are simple, that we have been taken in, deluded, and it's time we grew up?

There is a promise given by Jesus which is this: 'I am the light of the world. Whoever follows me will have the light of life and will never walk in darkness' (John 8:12). I am willing to trust his words above any other, dead or living!

I think back on my own life since I came to put my trust in Jesus: the things that have happened, the miracles which I have experienced at first hand—not just one or two, but many. I have seen people healed physically and mentally. I have seen people enter into a new relationship with God and with each other. I have seen broken lives, broken hearts, broken homes and broken communities mended. I have seen people come alive with hope and joy in seemingly hopeless conditions. I have seen people released from their fears and hang-ups, becoming strong and loving. I have seen the timid filled with power, given the ability beyond themselves to do the impossible. I have seen people die radiant, in their dying more alive than ever before, because their eyes were open to the joys to come. They 'saw the light'... And me? I can say, 'I have seen *the* light.' I can echo the man born blind, 'I was blind, now I can see.' I cannot prove it by logic or science; all I know is, I know that the One who is the light of the world is my light.

Yet how easy it is to lose sight of his light, to become short-sighted through sin, to be blinded by self-confidence, plunged into gloom and darkness by the infections of the world. We are all human; none of us has perfect vision—not this side of heaven—and we do well to pray constantly in the words of the collect at Evening Prayer:

Lighten our darkness,
Lord, we pray;
and in your mercy defend us
from all perils and dangers of this night;
for the love of your only Son,
our Saviour Jesus Christ. Amen.

Whose side are you on?

Matthew 6:24

Cup Final day at Wembley. The excitement has built up to fever pitch, the ground is crowded with those fortunate enough to have got a ticket, the place is a sea of blue and red, the fans resplendent in their club colours, with their scarves, hats, banners and rattles. No need to ask who they support, they proclaim it from head to toe! Then the cheers rise to a crescendo as the two teams run out on to the pitch, one side clad in the blue and white strip, the other in red and white. The referee blows his whistle and the Cup Final is underway.

For ninety minutes they battle it out, red versus blue, every man giving all he has for his side, being urged on by the fans, red for red, and blue for blue. For one team the joy of the Cup and the winners' medals; for the other side the disappointment of being runners-up—the losers. The fans share in the joy of their team, or the disappointment, but they will still wear the colours, win or lose; there will still be the 'welcome home' reception, because it is the team they support that matters, in good times and bad. No *real* fan changes sides.

I write feelingly! I have supported the same football team all my life. They have had times of great success and triumph, when the team members were household names, international stars. They have also had times in the doldrums, struggling, down a division, in real trouble—but they are my team, and I shall go on supporting them whatever happens to them. They are my chosen team, and I would never consider changing my allegiance.

That, of course, is 'just a game'; there are more important issues in life than who wins the match on Saturday afternoons. But the principle is the same, we have to make up our mind whose side we are on, and stick with it. In fact, there are only two sides to choose from, and although we would like to sit on the fence, it is impossible; it is one or the other.

Jesus put it like this to the crowd:

No one can be a slave of two masters; he will hate one and love the other; he will be loyal to one and despise the other. You cannot serve both God and money.

Those listening to him knew all about serving a master and about being a slave. They knew it meant no longer being able to make your own decisions, choosing what to do or when to do it. If you were a slave, your time was no longer your own. You were totally at your master's command; he decided what you did, and how and when. You belonged to him. Twenty-four hours a day, seven days a week, every year of your life, you were bound to him.

Of course, life for us is very different. We are not slaves, are we? It is not so many years, though, since people in this country were practically slaves to their employers. Nowadays, with a shorter working week, we spend perhaps only a quarter of our time working for someone else, the rest is ours. Yet we are bound to our employer. He pays our wages, so we in turn must give of our best, and be honest and loyal; we have a responsibility to him, and in turn he to us.

But what Jesus was talking about was not how we earn our living, but the motivation of our lives. He said, 'You cannot serve both God and money', and that applies equally to someone working on the assembly line in a factory, a teacher at the local comprehensive school, a mum at home with small children, a cabinet minister in Westminster, a checkout operator in the shopping-centre supermarket, a soldier serving in Northern Ireland or a student at a desk. We either serve God or ourselves; our motivation is either God-centred or self-centred.

As a teenager I was faced with that choice. I had been challenged by hearing a preacher say, 'There are only two ways you can go in life, God's way or your way'. At seventeen years old, just beginning to feel my feet in the world, with money in my pocket, time on my hands and opportunities galore, I was tempted to go my own way. No one was going to tell me what to do, I thought. I wanted to be the master of my own life, to do my own thing—and yet I knew deep down that I would make a mess of it if left to my own devices. Maybe I would make a lot of money, have a great deal of excitement, or travel the world, but that was not enough, not for a headstrong seventeen-year-old! The alternative was putting my life into God's hands, doing his will, even when it did not suit me, even when it would cost me, even when I would look and sound a fool to do so; and maybe that was the hardest thing of all, to be willing to be laughed at, to be thought of as soft. So I weighed up the 'pros and cons'. What were the advantages either way?

I saw the picture of the successful woman, the glittering prizes, the freedom; and against that I saw in my mind's eye a figure on a cross. He was looking at me very intently. It was a challenging, demanding look, but at the same time it was full of love and understanding. The cross was dark and rough, but tinged behind with golden sunlight, and that somehow took away the awfulness of the cross and gave it a glorious attractiveness. I made my choice there and then, a very definite choice, almost you could say in cold blood. I decided whose colours I would play in, whose side I was on, because I reckoned he offered the best sort of life. I recognized then, although only very simply and rather dimly, that the reason I had made that choice was because I knew that not only had I committed myself to God, to serve him all my days, but that he had committed himself to me. I could rely on him to get me through whatever came, and that was worth more than money in the bank, clothes on my back, time on my hands. I 'signed up' for life, and that for me was the start of real freedom.

O God, the author of peace
and lover of concord,
to know you is eternal life,
to serve you is perfect freedom.
Defend us your servants
from all assaults of our enemies;
that we may trust in your defence,

and not fear the power of any adversaries;
through Jesus Christ our Lord. Amen.

The evidence
is all around you

Matthew 6:25—34

Some years ago I saw a poster which said, 'Don't worry—it may never happen', and someone had scrawled across it, 'But it has—what do I do now?' The most banal words in the world are 'Don't worry'. And it is even more irritating when someone says to us, 'I wouldn't worry if I were you.' To which the answer is, 'I *am* worried, and I am *not* you.' Of course, people try to be kind when they see we are worried sick about something and when we are feeling depressed and anxious. They genuinely want to help, I am sure, but it really does not help one little bit. If anything, it makes matters worse, because then we feel they do not understand our situation, for if they did they would not say those useless words, 'Don't worry'.

What do we worry about? And let's face it, all of us do worry; it is common to all, rich and poor, young and old; more common than the common cold, more deadly than any known disease, because it is a killer. We worry about tomorrow, how we are going to manage, whether our money will spin out, if we can cope with the situation looming up before us, how we can face the person we must meet, what the result of the X-ray will reveal, whether we will have passed the exam—and so on, and so on. These situations are real enough, and can be multiplied a thousand times. I have only to walk down our High Street to know that that is true. I see young people lounging around, with no jobs or prospects, anxious-looking shoppers trying to make ends meet. I talk to people who are worried about their families, a marriage break-up, a child who is ill, or those pains which are getting worse and seem to be the ominous signs of something very serious. I see the headlines splashed across the newspaper stand, of outbreaks of violence, drug problems, road accidents. I hear the ambulance siren and wonder what has happened. Add to this the world problems which affect us all, for we do live in a global village, and what happens across the other side of the world has an almost immediate effect on our world right here at home—there are so many trouble spots, sensitive areas, 'high risk' places.

Why worry? We worry because we feel unable to cope with life and all its demands, for we live in a world where survival of the fittest is still seen to operate, and the weak are swept aside by the stream of rich and powerful.

The crowd listening to Jesus knew that was only too true. Most of them would be at the bottom of the pile; they were people under a foreign occupying power, ordinary folk dependent on their own brain and brawn to get them through; they lived in a very insecure world indeed—and Jesus says, 'Don't worry!' He asks them why they are worried, but unlike most people who say that, he goes on to give the answer. His are not pious platitudes, but a positive evaluation of the real situation. He says, look around, see the examples of nature, the birds in the sky, the wild flowers under your feet. Watch the relaxed way the birds fly, how they soar through the air, gently landing on earth. See the magnificent colours of the wild flowers, the delicate textures of the petals, shaped by a master craftsman, more beautiful than exotic silks, with fragrance thrown on the wind for all to enjoy.

This is why I tell you not to be worried about the food and drink you need in order to stay alive, or about clothes for your body. After all, isn't life worth more than food? And isn't the body worth more than clothes? Look at the birds flying around: they do not sow seeds, gather a harvest and put it in barns; yet your Father in heaven takes care of them! Aren't you worth much more than birds? Can any of you live a bit longer by worrying about it?

And why worry about clothes? Look how the wild flowers grow:
they do not work or make clothes for themselves. But I tell you
that not even King Solomon with all his wealth had clothes as
beautiful as one of these flowers. It is God who clothes the wild
grass—grass that is here today and gone tomorrow, burnt up in
the oven. Won't he be all the more sure to clothe you?
How little faith you have!

So do not start worrying: 'Where will my food come from? or my
drink? or my clothes?' (These are the things the pagans are al-
ways concerned about.) Your Father in heaven knows that you
need all these things. Instead, be concerned above everything else
with the Kingdom of God and with what he requires of you, and
he will provide you with all these other things. So do not worry
about tomorrow; it will have enough worries of its own. There is
no need to add to the troubles each day brings.

We too can enjoy the wonders of the earth and sky and sea. We
can be in the heart of a grimy city, and yet as we look up into the
sky see a graceful ballet of clouds, colour changes no film maker
could conceive, sunrise and sunset scenes more beautiful than
anything you could see in an art gallery. We can look out in the
depths of winter and see in the landscape of bare trees and frozen
furrows the greatest sculptures in the world. Have you ever looked
into a sparrow's nest and seen delicate eggs lying there, or picked
up a blackbird's feather, seen the sheen, felt the softness against
the spine? What about the banks of that despised weed, the dan-
delion, absolutely beautiful with a multitude of golden tongues
making up each flower. Then the daisies all around us, those little
white flowers tipped with pale pink or rich ruby red. We mow
them up without a thought, and yet pick one, look at it—it's a
jewel fit for a queen! 'All things bright and beautiful, the Lord God
made them all!'—and of course, that's the secret, the antidote to
worry. The Lord God made them all. He made us, and he sur-
rounds us with the evidence of his love. Oh yes, I know all about
the evil and the sorrow and the mess in the world. But that is the
result of our misuse of his gifts, our selfishness and sin—we must
take our responsibility, both individually and corporately.

When everything seemed to be going horribly wrong for Jesus, as the net closed in on him, and his friends began to realize that there was no easy way ahead, he told them, 'Do not be worried and upset.' What a thing to say! Of course they were worried and upset! But here's his answer: 'Believe in God and believe also in me... I am the way, the truth, and the life' (John 14:1, 6). Those who did believe him, who went his way, discovered the truth and came into an experience of real living. They found out what 'abundant life' meant, for they were to witness the greatest event in history. Jesus rose from the dead; they saw him, spoke to him, some even had their breakfast cooked by him. Then they were blessed by him and saw him leave the earth in triumph and glory, not as a dead corpse, but as a Living Lord, and they were filled with the power he had promised them so that they could go and share his message with others.

Have you ever seen those bright yellow badges with the words 'Smile—God loves you'? They make you smile back at them, and not just because of the bright yellow smiling face, but because it is so true. 'God loves you', and he has proved he does, because he has shown us his love, and goes on showing it to us day in, day out. He smiles at us, and it is the smile of a loving Father.

We can trust God. We can trust him with our lives, we can trust him with our money, our health, our family, our work, our world. What is the worst thing that can happen to us—that one thing we don't like to talk about, or even think about, because it worries us too much? It is death, described as 'the last enemy'. We try to disguise it in so many ways when it happens to someone we love. The undertaker quickly removes the body, we arrange the funeral as soon as we can, we send the clothes to the charity shop, burn the letters, and close the door. We speak of them as having 'passed away', 'gone to sleep'; we are afraid to say the word 'dead'. I mentioned this gently to a friend who had been bereaved, and who was using all sorts of strange words to describe death. She looked at me and said, 'I don't like that word, it sounds so final.' Yes, in one way it is, the final page of chapter one! But the future for the Christian is glorious—it is life for ever more, not an extension of this one, but a whole new dimension.

When a member of the Salvation Army dies, it is called 'promotion to glory'—I like that! For it is a real promotion, from the bottom division to the top, and it is certainly to glory, because it is to be with him who reigns in glory. God has our life, our death, and all the stages in between in his loving care. We can trust him, because he is our Father, and he takes responsibility for us. Our children don't worry about the next meal, or about their clothes, or about tomorrow—that's Dad's business; they are just busy getting on with life as members of the family. Our job is not to be worrying about tomorrow, what might or might not be, but putting our trust in God, getting on with the life he has given us, using it in the way he shows us.

I well remember being very ill at the birth of our first child. At one stage I began to panic, knowing that we were both in real danger, but then I remembered the words of the twenty-third Psalm, and as I said those words, 'The Lord is my shepherd,' the worry and anxiety ebbed away and in their place I knew peace and confidence—and, well, I am still here, and we have a fine son and daughter! Tomorrow, who knows what will happen? I don't, but God does, and I can trust him. I can trust him because I know him, and he has never let me down.

Recently, preaching in a Methodist chapel in West Yorkshire, I was speaking about my experience of God's love and care. I concluded by saying, '...and he has never let me down'—and from the congregation came a firm '...and he never will!' I looked at the man who had spoken. He was elderly, his face well lined. Our eyes met and we smiled at each other, for although we had never met before, we both knew the truth of what we had said. He apologized later for interrupting. 'I only wish I had more such interruptions,' I said.

'He never has... he never will.' We can rely on God our Father. He does know best; we can trust him. After all, look at the evidence!

> *He gave us eyes to see them,*
> *And lips that we might tell*
> *How great is God Almighty,*
> *Who has made all things well.*

Take a good look for yourself. And tomorrow? Well, that's another day.

Guilty, or not guilty?

Matthew 7:1—6

The young man walked with unsteady gait, at times wandering into the road, getting hooted and cursed at by passing motorists. Some people spoke to him to ask if he was all right, but his speech was slurred and they couldn't make out what he was trying to say. It was evident what was wrong with him: he was drunk. How disgusting, they thought, a young, good-looking fellow like that, rolling drunk in the middle of the day when he ought to have been working and earning his living. What a disgrace for his family! So they went on their way, shaking their heads at such behaviour, tut-tutting to themselves.

They didn't know, did they, that the young man was suffering from a progressive disease of the nervous system. That he had once earned his living. That he had a wife and two young children, and was desperate to be able to care for them and for himself. That he was trying to prove that he could go out on his own and could manage to walk and talk. That he was determined to get better, but sadly the disease was stronger than his spirit, and would get worse and worse until, little more than a cabbage, that young man would eventually die.

The hooting motorists, the indignant passers-by, didn't know the facts. They read the signs and passed their judgment—and were completely wrong.

What of the crowd listening to Jesus on the hillside? What judgment had they passed on him? Were they mentally ticking off points for and against him, based on the way he looked, the clothes he wore, the place he came from, the accent he spoke with, the friends he made? Did they compare him with other teachers they had heard, for style, delivery and content? What did they make of the other people packed in beside them listening to Jesus? Some looked rather silly, smelt a bit strong, seemed rather odd—what were they doing here? They didn't look the religious sort; what were they up to? Instant judgments were being made on that hillside sure enough, and then, almost as though Jesus was reading their thoughts, he said:

> *Do not judge others, so that God will not judge you, for God will judge you in the same way as you judge others, and he will apply to you the same rules you apply to others. Why, then, do you look at the speck in your brother's eye, and pay no attention to the log in your own eye? How dare you say to your brother, 'Please, let me take that speck out of your eye,' when you have a log in your own eye? You hypocrite! First take the log out of your own eye, and then you will be able to see clearly to take the speck out of your brother's eye.*

What about us? Do we make instant judgments on others? Do we allow our own preconceived ideas and prejudices to colour that judgment? Do we jump to conclusions without being in possession of all the facts? I do, and here I am jumping to conclusions, reckoning you do too! We are all armchair critics, sitting in judgment on our fellow men and women. Yet are we prepared to stand in their shoes, enter into their situation, be subject to their demands? We have no right to judge others, and yet we go on doing it.

Criticism kills the spirit of the one on the receiving end, diminishes him or her as a person, and can do lasting harm. So many people are handicapped in mind and spirit because of the way they were criticized as children, because a teacher or parent was continually pulling them to pieces, pointing out their weaknesses, instead of encouraging their strengths. I meet many people with terrible hang-ups because they were victims of unwarranted criticism in the past. It has almost destroyed them as people, and been a barrier to their being able to make stable relationships; the cloud still hangs over them, and hampers their freedom to be whole people today.

In these situations I have often found that the ministry of healing, through the laying on of hands with prayer, has been a means of releasing them from the blockages which have built up over the years; but how tragic that the damage was done in the first place by cruel and ignorant judgment being passed on them.

Jesus spoke very strongly indeed on the subject of judging others. He knew what an evil it was, and his warning words come to us: we stand under God's judgment if we continue in this judgmental attitude towards other people.

If we examine our attitudes towards others we will often find that the things we criticize most in others are the weaknesses in ourselves. I find people who are 'always right' irritate me beyond measure, and yet it is one of my characteristics; I do like to think I am right—every time! I get very cross when people forget to return books I have lent them, and then, on looking at my bookshelf, I see those I have failed to return. Just two ordinary and simple illustrations, but very revealing! Would I like God to judge me as I judge others? Could I bear it if he pushed aside my excuses, my pleadings? What hope would I have if he was to mark me on the same scale as I mark others? Yet Jesus says that if we judge others we stand in danger of the same judgment.

It is only as we see ourselves as we are, warts and all, and experience the love and forgiveness of God ourselves, that we then begin to see other people as lovable, forgivable, unique and special. We stand alongside them, for we are all equal at the foot of the cross; there is no room there for judgment, only for amazement at the love of God for us.

There is a strange note as Jesus finishes talking about the danger of passing judgment. He says:

> Do not give what is holy to dogs—they will only turn and attack you. Do not throw your pearls in front of pigs—they will only trample them underfoot.

It sounds out of place, and yet think about it. What is he talking about? Isn't it about the right sort of judgment—knowing when to share the things of the spirit with others; needing to have the gift of wisdom and discrimination in revealing God's dealings with us? In the book of Ecclesiastes we are told that there is a time for everything, and that includes 'the time for silence and the time for talk' (Ecclesiastes 3:7). There are things which are between us and God; they are sacred, and are his special gifts to us. How do we know what to share and what to keep? Ask any man or woman in love. Would they show off the gifts they have given one another? Probably yes, and they would be proud to do so: 'Look what he gave me...' but would they share with others their love letters, those personal, intimate tokens of love? I think not! It is a very delicate line between one and the other. There is a delicate balance also between what we share and what we keep to ourselves of God's dealings and gifts to us. We must pray for 'a right judgment in all things'—and be sensitive to the guidance of the Holy Spirit.

The Frankfurt Prayer dates back to the sixteenth century, but is just as valuable for us as we think about judgment, both silent and voiced:

Lord, the scripture says, 'There is a time for silence, and a time for speech.' Saviour, teach me the silence of humility, the silence of wisdom, the silence of love, the silence of perfection, the silence that speaks without words, the silence of faith. Lord, teach me to silence my own heart that I may listen to the gentle movement of the Holy Spirit within me, and sense the depths which are of God.

May we be kept from making unkind judgments, and from unwise speech.

You get what you ask for!

Matthew 7:7—12

Take any crowd, and I guarantee variety. There will be the 'dedicated to the cause' men and women, and also the inquisitive, the interested, the sceptics. You will find people who just see a crowd and join in. There may be hecklers and trouble-makers; the 'poking fun' brigade. There will be family parties, couples, groups of friends, gangs and loners. There will be enthusiasts and disinterested onlookers—'all sorts and conditions' of men and women, young and old. Whether it is a cricket match or a peace rally, Speakers Corner in Hyde Park or a village festival—people attract other people. And after all, what is a crowd but a lot of individuals who happen to be standing or sitting in close proximity?

Take the crowd listening to Jesus. They had come from all over the place: 'from Galilee and the Ten Towns, from Jerusalem, Judea, and the land on the other side of the Jordan' (Matthew 4:25). They had followed Jesus because they had heard him preaching, seen him healing, or had been told by others about this marvellous teacher and healer and so had decided to go along and hear and see for themselves. It was something to do, somewhere to go, and would provide them with a subject to talk about for many a long day. So, 'Come on, lads, let's see what's going on!'—they would bring the children, and the youngsters would run alongside, eager to be involved with whatever was happening, as a break from the boring routine of the village or town, a chance to enjoy new company, hear the gossip, or swap a few stories.

What were they looking for, hoping for? Some for nothing in

particular. Others, who had heard of the miracles Jesus had done, were looking for a miracle in their own life; probably they knew the chances were slim of a cure for their illness or disease, they knew from experience, by seeing others like themselves, that things could only get worse—that is, unless a miracle happened. There would be those who had brought along members of their family or friends who were in trouble, hoping to attract the attention of Jesus. And there would be many who were looking for some point to life, something to make it worth living, someone to pin their hopes on.

As Jesus looked at the crowd around him, he saw not just a sea of faces, but people who needed help—all kinds of help. He saw the family groups, with Dad in the centre, perhaps with a child on his shoulders or in his arms. He saw other men who had left the women and children at home to get on with the work while they had a day off, maybe fathers and grown sons together, enjoying each other's company. So he addressed himself to them:

Ask, and you will receive; seek, and you will find: knock, and the door will be opened to you. For everyone who asks will receive, and anyone who seeks will find, and the door will be opened to him who knocks. Would any of you who are fathers give your son a stone when he asks for bread? Or would you give him a snake when he asks for a fish? Bad as you are, you know how to give good things to your children. How much more, then, will your Father in heaven give good things to those who ask him!

'Would any of you...?' You can imagine the fathers in the crowd looking down at their children, or thinking of those at home as Jesus said those words. They knew it was true; they might not be perfect fathers, but when their children came to them, they did their best, tried to make sure the children had enough to eat, even when it meant giving to them off their own plate, a piece of bread, a little fish. Of course those fathers would give to them when they came asking, looking up, licking their lips in anticipation, holding out their little hands—they wouldn't push them away, or tease them, or hurt them. After all, these were their children; they had been responsible for bringing these little ones into the world; they loved them. So, Jesus reasoned with them, if that is how you respond to your children—and you are not all you ought to be by any means—surely God who is your Heavenly Father will be far more generous than you. You are his children, so go ahead and ask!

There are very few fathers who can resist the appeals of their own children, although sadly there are some. It is tragic when children have to be taken into care because of their parents' ill-treatment or neglect of them. We hear of child abuse and neglect, but those parents are scorned by society in general, regarded as unnatural. A man or woman who has abused a child, and particularly their own, has a very rough time indeed in prison from other prisoners, and quite often has to be kept in solitary confinement for their own protection. It is also true that, when children are in need, even the roughest and toughest people will rally round to help.

We all try to do the best for our children. The advertisers know this and play on our heart-strings, especially before Christmas; they know full well that when children come to their parents asking, 'Please can I have…?' if they go on long enough most parents will relent—because these are their children; they want them to be happy.

God is our Father, and so we can come to him with confidence asking for help. He wants us to ask, and delights to provide for us. The beginning of the book of Genesis tells of the joy God had in providing the glorious world for human beings to live in. The only trouble was, human beings messed it up. Again and again God rescued humanity, and gave them a fresh start—gave them everything, even his Son: 'For God loved the world so much that he gave his only Son, so that everyone who believes in him may not die but have eternal life' (John 3:16).

Do you believe this? Do you act as though you do? In Goole in Humberside there is a dockside Mariners' Club. The port missioner, Heinz Siedler, had plans for extensions which would give better facilities and more comfort for the seamen who came there from all over the world. He was explaining his plans to a businessman, who challenged Heinz, saying, 'But all this is going to cost a lot of money. Where will you get it from?' (He knew the club had only a small income.) Heinz said with a smile: 'Oh, that will be no problem. You see, I have a very rich Father!'

Some would say that Heinz was foolhardy. Others, myself included, know he was absolutely right—and that fine extended building bears testimony to his faith! Our Father in heaven wants us to ask for his help, and he wants us to trust him to help. Sometimes we get the first bit right and ask, but then we don't trust him to answer. Time after time, in my own experience, I have been put to shame by seeing God answer my plea for help so magnificently. The 'how much more...' has been more than I could ever have hoped for or imagined. I have known times of desperate tiredness when he has given me a new lease of life and not only got me through the situation, but given me an excess of energy. There have been times when I have gritted my teeth and asked, 'Just get me through this,' and he has given me in that situation carefree enjoyment. He does not dangle promises of something good before us and then whip them away, or exchange them for something inferior. He gives not only good gifts, but the best gifts—and there's the crux of it. We think we know just what we need, we plead for that particular thing, and we get something quite different. A disappointment? I have never found it to be so, it has always been so much better. If my prayers had always been answered in the way I wanted, or thought I wanted, I would have had a terrible time, and been in some dreadful situations. He is our Father, he gives good gifts; and protects us from being dazzled by the baubles which will only harm us if we clutch at them.

Jesus tells us to ask, to seek, to knock. Sometimes we have to go on asking for a long time, until we ask for the right thing. There are times when our searching takes us through very difficult and dangerous country. And we do not always knock at the right door. Remember the wise men who went knocking at Herod's door looking for Jesus—they lost their sense of direction when they took their eyes off the star and held a committee meeting instead.

God our Father gives only good gifts. He does not either send or give evil things—no stones or snakes, only bread and fish; good wholesome fare.

God is our Father, so it follows that we are all brothers and sisters. We also have a duty to respond to the call for help from the ones who look for guidance, who knock on our door. It is a very simple formula, positive and to the point:

Do for others what you want them to do for you: this is the meaning of the Law of Moses and of the teachings of the prophets.

Here, in a sentence, is the remedy for the world's ills, the answer to the problems in society; whether of unemployment in Europe, drought and famine in Africa, violence in Northern Ireland, or the continuing Israeli–Palestinian conflict. Put into practice, it would transform all human relationships, in politics, industry, education, law and order, the church and the family. It would revolutionize your life and mine. It would mean a new world, a peaceful world, a creative world.

The problem is, we interpret that sentence in a negative way, as 'I never do anyone any harm... I wouldn't hurt anyone.' I hear this said over and over again, but what it amounts to is passive indifference, which is not what Jesus is talking about at all.

The law tells us what we must not do; this affords protection for society. Jesus tells us what we must do; this is the way of freedom for all within our society, the positive way of living. When our children were small there were many arguments about who had the bigger piece of cake. However carefully I cut it in half for them, they complained bitterly that the other one had the bigger share. The answer was very simple, so simple it took me a long while to discover it. It was to allow one child to cut the cake, and the other one to choose which piece they had. No child would sell itself short!

If we learned to share our resources on the same principle, then no one would ask, or seek, or knock in vain, would they?

Only for the narrow-minded

Matthew 7:13—14

This is the age of unlimited choice; science and technology have seen to that. In the time it took to get from London to Edinburgh a few years ago, we can now wing our way right across the world, and the travel agents are hard pressed to find some new location for the holidaymakers, who have been everywhere—and probably more than once. Day trips to France, weekends in New York and short breaks in the Balearic Islands are commonplace; now we can trot off to the Far East for a week, explore the Canadian Rockies by rail, tramp along the Great Wall of China, cruise down the Nile. We have acquired a taste for foreign food, and even in the old traditional market towns in the north of England, Chinese takeaways stand side by side with the fish and chip shops and the local pub.

No longer do we have to wait for foods to be in season. We can have strawberries in January, or Brussels sprouts in May; all we have to do is take them out of the freezer. Walk round the super-market—the choice is overwhelming, with endless variations of everything imaginable, and we pile high our trolley with goods from the four corners of the earth.

Schools offer a bewildering choice of subjects for their pupils; it seems you can take an examination in just about everything, and follow it up with a degree. And there is scope for every sporting and leisure-time pursuit—and for the idle, endless TV pro-grammes to watch other people working, playing and entertaining.

The problem with so much variety available is that we are

constantly having to choose between one thing and another. It is permanently 'make your mind up time', and most of us tend to wander from one thing to another, never really settling down to one objective. We lack a sense of permanence, always looking for some new thing to take our interest. There may be nothing new under the sun, but there are endless variations on them!

The community in which we live and work, the places we visit on holiday, or the subjects we study for pleasure, all have an influence on our lives, as do the papers we read, the clubs we join, the friends we make. But what about life itself? Is it just one mad round, with endless diversions, until we finally drop off or out? Or are we really supposed to be heading somewhere? Is there one goal, one destination which is superior to all the rest?

As the famous Professor Joad used to say, 'It all depends on what you mean by...', and it does all depend on our view of 'life'. Is this life all there is? If so, then the best thing to do is get as much mileage out of it as possible—at as little cost as possible. 'Eat, drink, and be merry, for tomorrow...' Cram as much living into life as you can, try everything that comes your way; make sure you don't miss out on anything that's going.

What about the future, though? Is there anything beyond the grave? Many people think not. 'When you are dead you are dead,' they pronounce. Others are not so sure. They would like to hope there was something, but what sort of something? Well, that is the big question.

Most religions have some sort of 'hereafter'—often a shadowy place, a place of spirits, a rather frightening prospect. Others offer a chance of being swept into 'nothingness', or of becoming something or someone else and having 'another time around' here; it depends on how you lived this time whether that next 'other time around' will be better or worse than the last.

Jesus talked about 'life', about a life very different from a shadowy existence, or a re-run of this one. He talked of 'life in all its fullness', a life with God, as members of his family. We would not be going into that life unprepared, not knowing anything about it, fearful and lost; but as a child joyfully rushing home to see Dad, rather like breaking up for the holidays! More than this, Jesus himself would be there to welcome us home. He would be going on ahead, for as he promised, 'There are many rooms in my Father's house, and I am going to prepare a place for you. I would not tell you this if it were not so' (John 14:2).

All this sounds great. 'Two for the price of one'—one life now, and another to come... But there's more to it than that, because *we* make the decision whether we go or not. We have the choice—it's not an automatic 'pass in'.

Of course you may not agree with me—why should you? After all, there are many ways to the top of a mountain; it doesn't really matter which path you take, does it? Well, there may be many ways up a mountain, but if the person who has already done the journey says there is only one safe way, then I am inclined to take his word for it—I would be a fool to go against the advice of the expert. There have been a number of times in my life when, as a walker, I have asked the way somewhere, have been given the route and, looking at it, decided I knew better. I knew a quicker way, more easy on the legs, and definitely prettier! I have found to my cost that I was quite wrong and had to retrace my steps, and apologetically admit I should have taken the way I was instructed!

Jesus claimed to be *the* way, *the* truth and *the* life (John 14:6), and went on to say that no one comes to the Father but by him—that's quite some claim! For those who wanted to know the way, who had followed him up the hillside to hear about that way, he had this warning:

> Go in through the narrow gate, because the gate to hell is wide and the road that leads to it is easy, and there are many who travel it. But the gate to life is narrow and the way that leads to it is hard, and there are few people who find it.

Christians are often accused of being narrow-minded. I have that accusation thrown at me from time to time: 'You would be quite nice if you weren't so narrow-minded!' I can only reply to that, 'I admit I am narrow-minded, because Jesus was.' He was always reminding his friends that the narrow way was the way to life, and the broad way was the way to death. He pressed the point home over and over again. No wonder his followers were called 'people of *the Way*'. Now it makes sense to me that if Jesus went to all that trouble to warn people of the dangers of missing the road to God, then I ought to pay attention and, unlike on my walking trips, go the way I am told!

The ancient Israelites liked to wander around, even though they were warned over and over about the dangers. If you read the Old Testament, you will soon find out that when they went their own way they got into the most awful mess, and when they did as they were told by God they were safe. The trouble was, of course, they kept changing over and trying to have the best of both worlds. But it didn't work then—and neither can it now. Moses got very cross with the people. After all, God had appointed him as leader, and so he had to take the lead—but what a job! He made them face up to the decision:

Today I am giving you a choice between good and evil, between life and death. If you obey the commands of the Lord your God, which I give you today, if you love him, obey him, and keep all his laws, then you will prosper and become a nation of many people... I am now giving you the choice between life and death, between God's blessing and God's curse, and I call heaven and earth to witness the choice you make. Choose life. (Deuteronomy 30:15–16, 19).

Dramatic stuff! But then the situation was dramatic—life or death. And it still is.

So here I am, in a world filled with choice, able to pick and choose, to go this way or that. I make some mistakes, 'I win a few, lose a few'. But then, if one brand of beans is better than another, it doesn't really matter. If I choose to learn to paint or do flower-arranging, it won't alter my life all that much. If I go to Spain or Iceland for my holidays, either will be an experience. But the one choice I can't afford to make a mistake on is between heaven and hell, life or death—the words of Jesus, not mine. When it comes to decisions like that, I want to be sure!

John Bunyan in *Pilgrim's Progress* graphically describes the journey and the way.

> *Then said Evangelist, pointing with his finger over a very wide field, 'Do you see yonder wicket gate?' The man said, 'No.' Then said the other, 'Do you see yonder shining light?' He said, 'I think I do.' Then said Evangelist, 'Keep that light in your eye, and go up directly thereto, so shalt thou see the gate; at which when thou knockest it shall be told thee what thou shalt do.'*

Pilgrim had many adventures, many troubles, before he finally got to the end, but he kept on the narrow way, and he found life.

A latter-day pilgrim, Cardinal Basil Hume, in his book *To be a Pilgrim*, speaks of the way in these words:

> The way is often rough for a pilgrim and hard going, but pilgrims must keep going resolutely and courageously. They are lost if they stop looking for the right way to reach their destination. But there is one who is on the look-out to guide us; it is the Son of God, who is the way, the truth and the life.

The Cardinal finishes his book with a warning:

> It is possible to refuse to go to him. It is possible to deny him, to adore not him, but false gods, to hate him even. We can walk away deliberately. We can choose self, self alone, above and before all. We shall live on, barren, empty, miserable lives. That is hell.

Yes, this is all very narrow-minded stuff, isn't it? But then, if Jesus is right about the narrow way, it is the only way we can go.

Moses' advice was, 'Choose life'.

Jesus said, 'I am the way, the truth and the life.'

Only a fool would go the other way, wouldn't they?

Don't be taken in

Matthew 7:15—20

'Oh, grandma, what big eyes you've got!' ... 'All the better to see you with, my dear.'

'Oh, grandma, what big ears you've got!' ... 'All the better to hear you with, my dear.'

'Oh, grandma, what big teeth you've got!' ... 'All the better to eat you up...'

Fortunately, at this point little Red Riding Hood is rescued from the wolf who is masquerading as her grandma, dressed in grandma's clothes—of course, it's a fairy story, and as we know, it all works out in the end.

In real life there are plenty of wolves dressed up as innocent grandmas. The world is full of confidence tricksters who pretend to be what they are not, holding out false promises, playing the part of gentlemen (and women), having the right dress, accent and connections, looking all sweetness and light, but for one reason only, to deceive the innocent and take advantage of them. It is easy to get the trusting to part with their life's savings, the TV set, Uncle Bill's war medals, or what have you.

The confidence trick is one of the oldest tricks in the world. Rebecca aided her favourite son Jacob to deceive his father Isaac by making him appear hairy like his brother Esau, with a goatskin on his arms and wearing Esau's best clothes to have the feel and smell of him. Why go to all that trouble? So that Jacob could receive the blessing which was rightly Esau's—and it worked! A wife deceived a husband, a son his father. It's an account well worth reading, for it describes human nature today as much as then. It is surprising what people will do to obtain an advantage. It's all there in chapter 27 of the book of Genesis.

Sadly, it happens too in religious circles, for there are people who would deceive those looking for leadership and for guidance. Jesus warned his hearers about them when he said:

> *Be on your guard against false prophets; they come to you looking like sheep on the outside, but on the inside they are really like wild wolves. You will know them by what they do. Thorn bushes do not bear grapes, and briars do not bear figs. A healthy tree bears good fruit, but a poor tree bears bad fruit. A healthy tree cannot bear bad fruit, and a poor tree cannot bear good fruit. And any tree that does not bear good fruit is cut down and thrown in the fire. So then, you will know the false prophets by what they do.*

Yes, appearances can be very deceptive. There are self-styled prophets around today, with grand-sounding qualifications, self-awarded titles of Reverend, Pastor or even Bishop. They have the gift of oratory, leaving people spellbound with their preaching, able to use words of scripture to their own advantage. The cults shoot up like mushrooms, and seem to have a fatal fascination for young people in particular, who are looking for a leader, a faith, an ideal; depriving them not only of cash and possessions but, far more seriously, of their minds and hearts. There have been many tragic instances of young people falling for what seems so plausible, and giving their all for a lost cause. It is so easy to fall for emotional appeal; we all need to be on our guard, to use the minds that God has given us to examine the claims of those who seem to be offering *the* way.

There are many false prophets outside what we call mainstream Christianity—that is, outside the traditionally accepted denominations. They are usually most attractive, often wealthy, very aggressive in their missionary work and extremely convincing. They are successful for two main reasons, the first of which is that they have their salesmanship technique reduced to a very fine art; they have studied the psychology of human personality and know its weaknesses, and go for them. They are masters of persuasion.

The second reason they are so successful is that there is a widespread ignorance of what the gospel of Jesus Christ is really all about. We live today in a pagan situation. With the fall-off in Sunday schools, the lack of biblical teaching in schools, fewer parents taking their children to church, only a small minority know the basics of the Christian faith. We have now lost at least two generations, so we can no longer assume any biblical knowledge or understanding of Christian principles. Over and over again I have found in talking with people—and not only young people, but those of the post-war generations—a lack of any real contact with the church, apart from attending an occasional wedding or funeral. So of course the field is wide open for the wolves, even those very poorly disguised as sheep, to come in—the sad fact being that most people don't know the difference between a sheep and a wolf!

Even more serious is that within the church we have people who are respected and recognized as teachers and leaders, but who are also 'wolves in sheep's clothing'. There is a place, a very important place, in the church for theological discussion and questioning, but when the basic facts of Christian belief are called into dispute, denying biblical authority and traditional practice, then we should ask questions of the questioners, demand answers, and take a good look at their results.

Jesus said we can recognize a healthy tree by its healthy fruit, and vice versa. He instructed his hearers that the same principles applied to prophets—those who claimed to preach God's message. Look at the results, he said. Good advice! So let's look carefully at the results of the work of those who speak out with authority today. I look for evidence that people have recognized their sin, and done something about it—not only being sorry, but turning right away from it. I look for evidence that people have come to know God for themselves through meeting Jesus Christ, a living Saviour, and finding him a friend in need and also a Master to be obeyed. I look for people fired with love and enthusiasm to share what they have discovered, who know a power, not of themselves, but of God—the power of the Holy Spirit in their lives. I look for people who are putting into practice what Jesus said about loving others, caring for them, and sharing both materially and spiritually—goods and gospel! I look for people who are practising what they preach.

Am I looking for too much? Am I living in cloud-cuckoo land? I am forever being told that I am too idealistic, too definite, even too certain! I admit it. I am idealistic, definite and certain. This is because I constantly see lives being changed, people becoming different, new, alive; and I see what difference that makes in every area of their lives. I know it is possible. I know it is real.

I also see some people who are confused, unhappy, losing their spirit, losing their hope, as the result of paying attention to some of the teaching and views they have heard expressed. I see others, who were seeking for a faith to live by, turning away from the church, turning away in despair, because they feel that what is being offered isn't worth having—for it is no more than merely being told to pull themselves up by their own bootlaces, without being given any hope of doing so.

Look at the results of the prophets' teaching today, then decide if they are sheep or wolves! Don't be taken in by the look or sound of them, but go by the end product. Remember, like Isaac, you could be taken for a very expensive ride. So, as Jesus said, 'Be on your guard!'

Who are you?

Matthew 7:21—23

I was having a cup of coffee at the TV studio with someone who has become well known through a series he is in. Like most people in the entertainment business, he has had a long struggle making it to the top, but now he is doing well, the series is a success, and he is enjoying being in great demand. 'It's funny,' he said, 'how many friends you suddenly find you have when things go well. The letters I get from folk who claim to be old pals breezily call me by my Christian name, say how they would like to meet up with me again... and then ask for favours! And I've never heard of them!' He grinned and went on, 'And there's some I remember who wouldn't have given me change for a tanner when it was tough a few years back, and now they come the bosom pal act!'

It is a trait of human nature that if someone gets on in the world, makes a name for themselves, comes into money, there are plenty of people who try the 'remember me?' line.

Jesus knew all about the 'remember me?' line. He knew that many would hope to work that one on him, so he gave them a warning:

Not everyone who calls me 'Lord, Lord' will enter the Kingdom
of heaven, but only those who do what my Father in heaven
wants them to do. When Judgment Day comes, many will say to
me, 'Lord, Lord! In your name we spoke God's message, by your
name we drove out many demons and performed many

miracles!' Then I will say to them, 'I never knew you. Get away
from me, you wicked people!'

A very strong warning indeed! Jesus does not want people to get
a false idea of what entering the Kingdom of heaven depends on.
He knew there would be many who would think it was enough to
have cheered him on his way at some time, to have gasped with
amazement at a miracle, or applauded his exchanges with the
scribes or Pharisees. There would be those, too, who would use
his name for their own purposes, and consider that was the entrance ticket to the Kingdom of heaven.

C.H. Dodd, in his book *The Parables of the Kingdom*, says:

> *Jesus had to say to would-be followers, The treasure is within
> your reach; but what will you pay for it? Not that the blessings of
> the Kingdom of God can be bought at any price: they are the gift
> of God. But because the situation called for sacrifice, it raised the
> question at issue to the point at which nothing short of absolute
> sincerity would count. 'Will you accept the Kingdom of God?'
> meant, in view of the facts, 'Will you stake your life upon it?' ...
> So the multitudes who were brought by the preaching of Jesus
> within the scope of the Kingdom of God were sifted by the way in
> which things went. They passed judgment upon themselves...*

All of us are under judgment, and face a Judgment Day when all
will be revealed. It would be pleasant to imagine that this will not
happen, that like all good fairy stories 'they live happily ever after'.
But life is not a fairy story where the writer manipulates the char-
acters so that everyone finishes up a 'goodie'. Life is the gift of
God to each one of us, and we will be called to account for the
way we have used it. I have a constant reminder of this in my
kitchen where I have stuck on the wall a poster which says, 'What
you are is God's gift to you. What you become is your gift to God.'
It is a two-way thing, giving and receiving! I need to be reminded
of that fact, otherwise I can soon get a very false idea of what I am
supposed to be about.

Of course, we may have given this some thought, and so we
'clock in' Sunday by Sunday at church, put our hands into our
pockets when the plate comes round and stick in a couple of
pounds. We may serve on the Church Council or Elders Group,

or on one of the many and varied committees that are within the church. We may be prepared to roll up our sleeves and get stuck into the jobs that need doing, like cleaning out the gutters, washing the choir robes, polishing the brass or making the tea at one of those endless meetings. We may see a bit further than the local church and be involved in the Synod, standing up and making speeches about 'critical issues facing the church today'; we may even write a book or two about such things. It could be that we 'go into the church', turn our collars round, wear a cassock, have charge of a church, and do all the things expected of us, and are very good at them too, not least in reminding God of our interest in his affairs and of our participation.

It could be that at the Day of Judgment, when we arrive confidently, knowing we have a good track record, we will hear the words, 'I never knew you!'

Jesus says it is not just saying 'Lord, Lord' that counts, but doing what God wants us to do. Obedience to what God commands—but what does he ask us? He was once asked what was the most important commandment, and he said this:

> 'Love the Lord your God with all your heart, with all your soul, with all your mind, and with all your strength. The second most important commandment is this: Love your neighbour as you love yourself. There is no other commandment more important than these two.'

> The teacher of the Law said to Jesus,
> 'Well done, Teacher! It is true, as you say, that only the Lord is God and that there is no other god but he. And man must love God with all his heart and with all his mind and with all his strength; and he must love his neighbour as he loves himself. It is more important to obey these two commandments than to offer animals and other sacrifices to God.'

> Jesus noticed how wise his answer was, and so he told him, 'You are not far from the Kingdom of God.'

> After this, nobody dared to ask Jesus any more questions.
> (Mark 12:30–34)

Jesus said that the man was 'not far from the Kingdom of God'. To enter that kingdom, though, he would have to put his belief into practice. To love God and to love people is not something we organize, but a relationship we come into; it is a response with every bit of our being. As a husband and wife give themselves to each other in love, so we give ourselves to God and to his service. It is a 'labour of love', and will alter our attitude to worship, to work, to everything we do. We will feed the hungry, care for the strangers, visit the sick, comfort the sad, love the unlovable. We will respond to human need without a second thought, because we love people and want the very best for them, not because we are looking for gratitude or acclaim.

Of course, we get things wrong so often, we make many mistakes. But if our hearts are right, then we will do what is right. Paul, writing to the Corinthians, spelled it out very clearly that, whatever our gifts and abilities and actions, unless we are motivated by love they are worth absolutely nothing. 'If I have no love, this does me no good' (1 Corinthians 13:3), but 'love is eternal' and lasts for ever.

Yes, love lasts for ever, and we are on the receiving end of the love of God for ever, starting now. As C.H. Dodd says, 'Such blessedness may be enjoyed here and now, but it is never exhausted in any experience that falls within the bounds of time and space.'

On the Day of Judgment, if we have already entered into that relationship with God in Jesus, if we have responded to his love by giving ourselves to him in love, we won't have to plead 'Lord, Lord.' We won't have to say, 'Remember me?' There will be instant recognition.

Recently at Kings Cross station in London, as I was walking from the train to the exit, a sailor pushed past me. I was a bit irritated until I saw why. Running towards him was a girl, his wife or girlfriend, I don't know, but as they met he gathered her up into his arms, and there they stood, oblivious to everything and everybody around them. As I walked past, a man turned to me and said, 'Ain't love wonderful!'

The kingdom of heaven is entered into now, through coming into that love relationship with Jesus, and lived out in loving obedience. It is not a matter of what we say, but of whose we are.

Then the Day of Judgment holds no fear.

> *Love divine, all love excelling,*
> *Joy of heaven, to earth come down,*
> *Fix in us Thy humble dwelling,*
> *All Thy faithful mercies crown:*
>
> *Changed from glory into glory,*
> *Till in heaven we take our place;*
> *Till we cast our crowns before Thee,*
> *Lost in wonder, love and praise.*

(Charles Wesley)

Or, in the words of my fellow rail traveller, 'Ain't love wonderful!'

Built to last

Matthew 7:24—27

'Communication' is the 'in' word of our age. The technical advances in the field of communication over the last few years are both wonderful and fearful. One sophisticated system is rapidly outstripped by another; the most intricate method soon becomes mere child's play.

There are few homes today without at least one TV set; they can equally be found in kitchen and bedroom, as well as presiding over the living-room. Soon they will come as just another fitment, like bathroom tiles to match the curtains. Apart from a few hours between the late night film and Breakfast TV, we have a continual bombardment of pictures, and now with video those hours can be filled with films, or reruns of programmes previously recorded. We now have a multitude to choose from via satellite, and some of us do not even need to move from our chair to do our shopping, banking or worshipping. The computer has taken over from notepad and order form, with e-mail and the Internet fast replacing conventional mailing systems.

We still read, of course, but now books are no longer lasting treasures, but disposable paperbacks, whose brightly coloured covers attract the attention more than leather-bound volumes. Magazines get glossier, newspapers are little more than headlines with pictures, because we will no longer bother to plod through the pages to find out what has happened, we want it instantly to hand.

Pictures, sounds, words, all rush in at us, demanding to be seen, heard, read. Instant information on every topic under the sun—and beyond—is ours. The trouble is, we see, hear and read, and yet so often cannot recall anything. It is a case of 'in one ear (or eye) and out the other'. It is 'moving wallpaper' of varying colour and shade and tone. My fear is that the time will come when we are so bombarded with information that we will no longer be capable of making a choice, or acting upon the information we have received; the sheer volume will crowd out response.

Yet is this so new? When Jesus told the parable of the Sower, which is recorded for us in Matthew, Mark and Luke, he was drawing attention to the fact that words are like seeds being scattered and, for a variety of reasons, failing to take root, failing to bring any result. Today words are sown so densely that they crowd each other out; few can take root because of the sheer volume.

What about the crowd who listened to Jesus? No distractions for them; they could give their total concentration to what he was saying—or could they? What ideas, memories, feelings crowded in upon them as they sat listening to Jesus? Just like us as we sit in church, eyes fixed upon the preacher and yet so often far away, our minds filled with other places, other people, other words. Jesus warned his hearers about the danger of merely hearing his words and failing to act upon what they had heard.

Jesus was the greatest of communicators. He needed no microphone, overhead projector, or visual presentation pack. He drew upon scripture, the Word of God. He pointed to the ordinary things of life, like seeds and water, flowers and wind. He drew his illustrations from the daily life of a working man, his sheep and oxen; from a woman's ornaments, her personal treasures. He started from where people were, with the things they knew and understood, and opened up through them the treasures of heaven, the perils of hell.

As he came to the end of the Sermon on the Mount, he knew that the great danger for those who had listened to his every word was the likelihood that, having heard what he had to say, having seen the importance of what he had told them, they would do... absolutely nothing. They would return home, back to everyday life, and gradually the memory of the time they had listened to him would be eroded away by new experiences, voices, demands, pleasures. So he painted the picture for them of a situation they would know so well; of a builder, building his house. Of the right way to do it, and the wrong way, and of the consequences.

So then, anyone who hears these words of mine and obeys them is like a wise man who built his house on rock. The rain poured down, the rivers overflowed, and the wind blew hard against the house. But it did not fall, because it was built on rock.

But anyone whose hears these words of mine and does not obey them is like a foolish man who built his house on sand. The rain poured down, the rivers overflowed, and the wind blew hard against that house, and it fell. And what a terrible fall that was!

House-building technique has not changed all that much since the time of Jesus. In many parts of the world the basic design can still be seen. And our own home, be it a modern 'semi', cottage, flat or 'ancient monument', may have all sorts of refinements—double glazing, central heating, wall-to-wall carpeting and floor-to-ceiling tiling—but it is still basically a box to shelter in. What matters is that within it we are secure, protected from the elements, able to make that box into a home, somewhere to go out from and come into; somewhere to belong.

Jesus says that if we hear what he has to say and obey him, then we will be safe, whatever happens. He does not say that the rain will not pour down, or the wind blow; in fact we can assume that it will—the storms come upon us as they come upon the man next door. We all experience times when everything seems impossible, when darkness is upon us day and night, when we feel totally alone and isolated. I know only too well by experience that awful 'dark night of the soul'. There are times when the waters of sorrow, pain, and anxiety almost sweep us away. But the promise is that if we listen to Jesus, if we obey him, then we are safe and sound. The psalmist knew that given confidence in God, for he could say, 'He set me safely on a rock and made me secure' (Psalm 40:2).

We are called to build our lives on that firm foundation. Paul says, writing to the Christians in Ephesus, 'You, too, are built upon the foundation laid by the apostles and prophets, the cornerstone being Christ himself' (Ephesians 2:20). We hear Jesus' instructions, are given the 'blueprint', and then we are to follow them out.

Of course, we may be content simply to listen to what Jesus says, nod our heads in approval, and give him a vote of confidence. But in that case we are building on shifting sand, for there is no substance to a nod of approval, or a hand raised in a crowd, unless it is followed up with action.

In the history of our parish church, one man stood out above the rest; he was called Samuel Froggatt. He was obviously a great preacher, for whenever I talk to an old person in our town they will invariably tell me about the time they heard Samuel Froggatt. In his day you had to come to church early if you wanted a seat. Every service was packed, every meeting filled, and they sigh with pleasure at the memory of Samuel Froggatt. Many came to faith in Jesus Christ through his ministry and served him all their lives; but many more heard Samuel Froggatt preach the good news of Jesus Christ, applauded the message and the messenger, but did nothing about it. What good will it be to say to God, 'I heard Samuel Froggatt preach'? Won't the question be, 'What did you do about it?' And we may have to say, 'Not a lot'—in actual fact, nothing at all.

Perhaps the saddest words that are ever said are, 'If only I had...' I hear those words said so often, something after a tragedy or a bereavement. But it is too late, the opportunity has passed. It is so easy to be wise after the event. With that wisdom of after-thought comes remorse, guilt, despair, and as people say those words through their tears, 'If only I had...', it seems as though I hear falling masonry, the splitting of timbers, and the shattering of glass; and I remember the picture Jesus painted of the house on the sand, his description of its destruction in the storm, and his words, '...and what a terrible fall that was!'

The Sermon on the Mount finishes with the warning that unless we do something about the words Jesus speaks, we are as stupid as a man building a house on shifting sand.

How fortunate we are, because we have been warned of the danger. We can do something about our lives. We have the opportunity, now we have heard, to put his words into practice. That is, so long as we do not go on putting off taking action. Because if we do, we also may one day be saying, 'If only I had...' But then, it will be too late.

By whose authority?

Matthew 7:28—29

When I worked in industry, there were two managers whom I remember well. One was determined that everyone should know he was in charge, and so he took to himself the trimmings of what he considered management was all about. He arrived dead on nine o'clock. He made his entrance with a flourish, barking orders as he came. He wore a dark suit, white shirt and college tie, and his shoes were always immaculate. His desk was laid out with military precision to make sure he was seen to be 'managing', and he had his paper qualifications framed and in a prominent place, along with graphs and flow charts which proved his expertise. Yet he might as well not have been there for all the notice anyone took of him. Oh yes, people said what was expected of them, and took care to be working when he inspected the departments. But in spite of the trappings of management, he carried no weight of authority.

The other one was a fatherly figure. He was always around; he arrived before anyone else, and was the last to leave. His desk was organized chaos, and his door was always open to whoever wanted to come and see him. He ambled round the mill in a rather crumpled tweed suit. He knew everybody, and was concerned about their families, their hobbies, their worries. He could turn his hand to any job in the mill, and was not afraid to get his hands dirty. He never seemed to be in a hurry. He didn't miss a trick and he never needed to raise his voice. His authority was recognized and respected. It was never questioned, for it was not something he tried to acquire, he just had it.

William Barclay said this of the authority of Jesus:

> *When Jesus spoke, he spoke as if he needed no authority be-*
> *yond himself. He spoke with utter independence. He cited no au-*
> *thorities and quoted no experts. He spoke with the finality of the*
> *voice of God. To the people it was like a breeze from heaven to*
> *hear someone speak like that. The terrific, positive certainty of*
> *Jesus was the very antithesis of the careful quotations of the*
> *scribes. The note of personal authority rang out—and that is a*
> *note which captures the ear of every man. (The Gospel of Mark)*

A modern man looks at the person of Jesus, and comes to the conclusion that he spoke with the voice of God. But what about the
crowd who heard him, sitting on the hillside? What impression
did he make on them?

> *When Jesus finished saying these things, the crowd was amazed*
> *at the way he taught. He wasn't like the teachers of the Law;*
> *instead, he taught with authority.*

The crowd were amazed because here was someone not interpret-
ing the past in an academic manner, but taking it and saying, 'This
has now come to pass.' As when he read from the prophet Isaiah:

> *The Spirit of the Lord is upon me,*
> *because he has chosen me to bring good news to the poor.*
> *He has sent me to proclaim liberty to the captives*
> *and recovery of sight to the blind;*
> *to set free the oppressed*
> *and announce that the time has come*
> *when the Lord will save his people.*

He went on to say, 'This passage of scripture has come true today,
as you heard it being read' (Luke 4:18–21). What preacher could
stand up and say that today? However brilliant his sermon, he
would be dismissed as a crank or a lunatic, making a claim like
that! Ridicule or pity would be the response to such wild claims.

Those who heard Jesus were amazed at his words. They accepted them because they recognized that he spoke with authority, unlike those who merely reiterated what others had said before
them, rehashing the old examination papers, polishing up the

points. Jesus was pointing to the future, opening up a new and living way, so that men and women could discover that God was their Father, that his kingdom was theirs. Entrance was free to everyone, but it would cost them everything they had. It would cost them their hearts and minds and wills.

Two thousand years have gone by since Jesus preached the most famous sermon of all time, and it still speaks with devastating accuracy to our condition today. 'If only people today lived by the Sermon on the Mount, the world would be a better place.' Yes, my fellow traveller, it would be! So what are you going to do? If you agree that what Jesus said was right, if you agree that he has the authority to say what he said, then you have to do something... like changing your way of life, your attitudes. The ball is in your court.

It is so easy for us to be carried away with the words and ideals, to enjoy the atmosphere of them, and forget the warning that comes with them. To hear is not enough. To agree is insufficient. Jesus calls for immediate action and for our wholehearted obedience—and there is no substitute for either.

The Bible is not simply great literature to be admired and revered; it is Good News for all people everywhere—a message both to be understood and to be applied in daily life. (Preface to the Good News Bible)

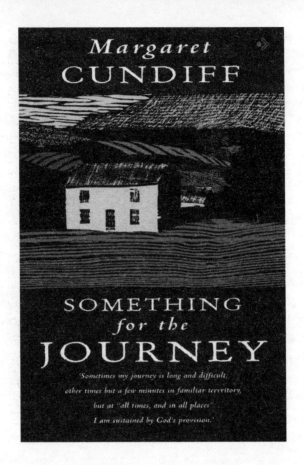

The Bible is full of gifts for us—expressions of God's love and concern which help sustain our faith. This book reflects in 'Thought for the Day' style on some of those gifts—some of the well-loved Bible verses shared by friends and fellow Christians with each other.

£5.99, ISBN 1 84101 025 1

Available from your local Christian bookshop or, in case of difficulty, direct from BRF.

Margaret Cundiff is a regular contributor to *New Daylight*, the Bible Reading Fellowship's popular series of daily Bible reading notes. Published three times a year, in January, May and September, priced at £2.70 per issue, *New Daylight* is available from your local Christian bookshop or, in case of difficulty, direct from BRF.

New Daylight is also available in a large print edition, or on audio cassette. For further details, contact BRF.

Tel: 01865 748227; fax: 01865 773150;
e-mail: enquiries@brf.org.uk